rockschool®

Guitar
US Level 6 (UK Grade 6)

Performance pieces, technical exercises and in-depth guidance for Rockschool assessments

All accompanying and supporting audio can be downloaded from: *www.rslawards.com/downloads*

Input the following code when prompted: **F7AS4KTK62**

For more information, turn to page 4

www.rslawards.com

Acknowledgements

Published by Rockschool Ltd. © 2012, 2018 & 2020
Catalogue Number: RSK200048US
ISBN: 978-1-78936-144-5
Initial US Release | Errata details can be found at *www.rslawards.com/errata*

CONTACTING ROCKSCHOOL
www.rslawards.com
Telephone: +44 (0)345 460 4747
Email: *info@rslawards.com*

Syllabus Director
Tim Bennett-Hart

Head of Graded Music & Publishing
Jono Harrison

2018 Syllabus Repertoire
Produced by Nik Preston

Proof reading
Sharon Kelly, Calum Harrison, Jono Harrison, Nik Preston
(and all arrangers/performers)

US Book Editions (2020)
Additional design work by Steven Price (51 Degrees Design)
and Simon Troup (Digital Music Art)
Edited by Jennie Troup (Digital Music Art)

Syllabus Consultants (Hit Tunes 2018 Repertoire)
Guitar: James Betteridge, Andy G Jones
Bass: Joe Hubbard, Diego Kovadloff, Joel McIver
Drums: Paul Elliott, Pete Riley

Arrangers (Hit Tunes 2018 Repertoire)
Guitar: James Betteridge, Andy G Jones, Mike Goodman, Viv Lock
Bass: Diego Kovadloff, Andy Robertson, Joe Hubbard
Drums: Paul Elliott, Stu Roberts, Pete Riley

Publishing (Hit Tunes 2018 Repertoire)
Fact files by Diego Kovadloff
Covers designed by Phil Millard (Rather Nice design)
Music engraving, internal design and layout by
Simon Troup & Jennie Troup (Digital Music Art)

Distribution
Exclusive Distributors: Hal Leonard

Musicians (Hit Tunes 2018 Repertoire)
Guitar: Andy G Jones, James Betteridge, Mike Goodman,
   David Rhodes (Peter Gabriel)
Bass: Nik Preston, Joe Hubbard, Stuart Clayton,
   Andy Robertson, John Illsley (Dire Straits)
Drums: Paul Elliott, Pete Riley, Peter Huntington, Stu Roberts,
   Billy Cobham (Miles Davis, Mahavishnu Orchestra)
Vocals: Kim Chandler
Keys: Jono Harrison, Hannah V (on 'Red Baron'), Andy Robertson
Horns: Tom Walsh (tpt), Martin Williams (sax), Andy Wood (trmb)

Recording & Audio Engineering (Hit Tunes 2018 Repertoire)
Recording engineers: Oli Jacobs, Scott Barnett, Patrick Phillips
Mixing engineer: Samuel Vasanth
Mastering engineer: Samuel Vasanth
Audio production: Nik Preston
Audio management: Ash Preston, Samuel Vasanth
Recording studios: Real World Studios, The Premises

Publishing (Rockschool 2012 Repertoire)
Fact Files written by Joe Bennett, Charlie Griffiths, Stephen Lawson,
Simon Pitt, Stuart Ryan and James Uings
Walkthroughs written by James Uings
Music engraving, internal design and layout by
Simon Troup & Jennie Troup (Digital Music Art)
Proof reading and copy editing by Chris Bird, Claire Davies, Stephen
Lawson, Simon Pitt and James Uings
Publishing administration by Caroline Uings
Additional drum proof reading by Miguel Andrews

Instrumental Specialists (Rockschool 2012 Repertoire)
Guitar: James Uings
Bass: Stuart Clayton
Drums: Noam Lederman

Musicians (Rockschool 2012 Repertoire)
Andy Crompton, Camilo Tirado, Carl Sterling, Charlie Griffiths,
Chris Webster, Dave Marks, DJ Harry Love, Felipe Karam,
Fergus Gerrand, Henry Thomas, Jake Painter, James Arben,
James Uings, Jason Bowld, Joe Bennett, Jon Musgrave, Kishon Khan,
Kit Morgan, Larry Carlton, Neel Dhorajiwala, Nir Z, Noam Lederman,
Norton York, Richard Pardy, Ross Stanley, Simon Troup, Steve Walker,
Stuart Clayton, Stuart Ryan

Recording & Audio Engineering (Rockschool 2012 Repertoire)
Recorded at The Farm (Fisher Lane Studios)
Produced and engineered by Nick Davis
Assistant engineer and Pro Tools operator Mark Binge
Mixed and mastered at Langlei Studios
Mixing and additional editing by Duncan Jordan
Supporting Tests recorded by Duncan Jordan and Kit Morgan
Mastered by Duncan Jordan
Executive producers: James Uings, Jeremy Ward and Noam Lederman

Executive Producers
John Simpson, Norton York

Table of Contents

Introductions & Information

- 1   Title Page
- 2   Acknowledgements
- 3   Table of Contents
- 4   Welcome to Rockschool Guitar Level/Grade 6

Hit Tunes

- 5   Breakestra .... 'Cramp Your Style'
- 9   Alicia Keys .... 'If I Ain't Got You (Live)'
- 15   Jill Scott .... 'The Real Thing/The Way (Live)'
- 21   Soundgarden .... 'Fell On Black Days'
- 27   Prince .... 'I Wanna Be Your Lover'
- 33   Cream .... 'Crossroads'

Rockschool Originals

- 39   'Mohair Mountain'
- 45   'Striped Shirt'
- 49   'That Sounds Like Noise'
- 55   'Blue Espresso'
- 61   'Cranial Contraption'
- 67   'Favela'

Technical Exercises

- 73   Scales, Modes, Arpeggios, Chords and Stylistic Studies

Supporting Tests

- 77   Quick Study Piece
- 80   Ear Tests
- 81   General Musicianship Questions

Additional Information

- 82   Entering Rockschool Assessments
- 83   Marking Schemes
- 84   Introduction to Tone
- 86   Guitar Notation Explained
- 87   Mechanical Copyright Information
- 88   Rockschool Popular Music Theory

Welcome to Rockschool Guitar Level/Grade 6

Welcome to Guitar Level/Grade 6
Welcome to the **Rockschool 2018 Guitar syllabus**. This book and the accompanying downloadable audio contain everything you need to play guitar at this level/grade. In the book you will find the scores in both standard guitar notation and TAB, as well as Fact Files and Walkthroughs for each song.
The downloadable audio includes:
- full stereo mixes of six Rockschool compositions and six arrangements of classic and contemporary hits
- backing tracks (minus the assessed guitar part)
- all necessary audio for the complete range of supporting tests

Guitar Assessments
At each level/grade, you have the option of taking one of two different types of assessment:

- **Level/Grade Assessment:** a Level/Grade Assessment is a mixture of music performances, technical work and tests. You prepare three pieces (two of which may be Free Choice Pieces) and the contents of the Technical Exercise section. This accounts for 75% of the assessment marks. The other 25% consists of: a Quick Study Piece (10%), a pair of instrument specific Ear Tests (10%), and finally you will be asked five General Musicianship Questions (5%). The pass mark is 60%.

- **Performance Certificate:** in a Performance Certificate you play five pieces. Up to three of these can be Free Choice Pieces. Each song is marked out of 20 and the pass mark is 60%.

Book Contents
The book is divided into a number of sections. These are:

- **Assessment Pieces:** in this book you will find six specially commissioned pieces of Level/Grade 6 standard. Each of these is preceded by a *Fact File*. Each Fact File contains a summary of the song, including the style, tempo, key and technical features, along with a list of the musicians who played on it. The song is printed on up to four pages. Immediately after each song is a *Walkthrough*. This covers the song from a performance perspective, focusing on the technical issues you will encounter along the way. Each song comes with a full mix version and a backing track. Both versions have spoken count-ins at the beginning. Please note that any solos played on the full mix versions are indicative only.

- **Technical Exercises:** you should prepare the exercises set in this level/grade in the keys indicated. You should also choose *one* Stylistic Study from the three printed to practise and play to the backing track in the assessment. The style you choose will determine the style of the Quick Study Piece.

- **Supporting Tests and General Musicianship Questions:** in Guitar Level/Grade 6 there are three supporting tests – a Quick Study Piece, a pair of Ear Tests and a set of General Musicianship Questions (GMQs) asked at the end of each assessment. Examples of the types of tests likely to appear in the assessment are printed in this book. Additional examples of both types of test and the GMQs can be found in the Rockschool *Guitar Companion Guide*.

- **Additional Information:** finally, you will find information on assessment procedures, marking schemes, guitar tone, guitar notation, and the full notation and backing track of a piece from the next level/grade as a taster.

Audio
Audio is provided in the form of backing tracks (minus guitar) and examples (including guitar) for the pieces and the supporting tests where applicable. Audio files are supplied in MP3 format to enable playback on a wide range of compatible devices. Digital versions of the book include audio files in the download. Download audio for hardcopy books from RSL directly at *www.rslawards.com/downloads* — you will need to input this code when prompted: **F7AS4KTK62**

Syllabus Guide
All candidates should read the accompanying syllabus guide when using this level/grade book. This can be downloaded from the RSL website: *www.rslawards.com*

Errata
Updates and changes to Rockschool books are documented online. Candidates should check for errata periodically while studying for any assessment. Further details can be found on the RSL website: *www.rslawards.com/errata*

Breakestra

SONG TITLE: CRAMP YOUR STYLE
ALBUM: SINGLE RELEASE 1972
LABEL: RELATIVITY
GENRE: FUNK

WRITTEN BY: WILLIE G. HALE
PRODUCED BY: W. CLARKE
AND STEVE ALAIMO

US CHART PEAK: N/A

BACKGROUND INFO

'Cramp Your Style' was released as a single on the Blue Candle label in 1972. The Breakestra version is included on Thievery Corporation's compilation *The Outernational Sound*, released in 2004.

Breakestra are a funk collective based in Los Angeles. They specialise in playing an A to Z of funk classics true to style. They are led by vocalist and bassist Miles Tackett who is also a producer.

The Thievery Corporation are a DJ/Producer duo who have a rotating cast of musicians on their live sets. They formed in 1995 and they have an interest in music from all over the world, with particular emphasis on Brazilian and Jamaican music. They have released 10 studio albums and 18 compilations. Rob Garza and Eric Hilton (Thievery Corporation) also run the Eighteenth Street Lounge Music label and have performed all over the world.

Cramp Your Style

Breakestra
Words & Music by Willie Hale

Walkthrough

Amp Settings

The song was recorded on a Stratocaster type guitar, set to the neck pickup. The amp was set to the overdrive channel with a medium amount of gain for a 'crunchy' overall tone. Depending on the type of guitar and amp you play through these suggested amp settings will change.

Try experimenting with the levels of Bass, Middle and Treble and see what you prefer. Experiment with pickup selection and tone controls on the guitar and see what different tonal colours you like and feel suit the sound of the song the best.

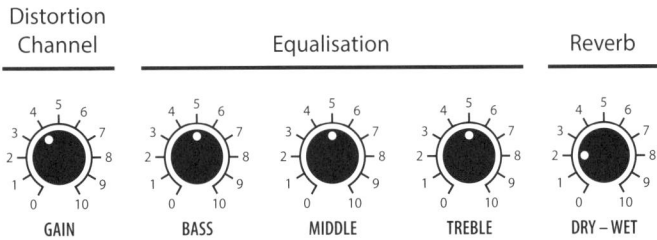

Intro

This bluesy/funk track is in the key of F# and begins with an eigh-measure single note riff (originally played by a saxophone). The riff starts with semitone movement, hammering on and pulling off from a C and C# (5th), then to F to F# (Root). Focus on getting a smooth legato sound here. At measure 5 the guitar plays dominant 7th chords, descending in 4ths, starting on F#^{7} (tonic) to B^7 (IV^7), E^7 ($\flat$VII^7), A^7 ($\flat$III^7), finishing on a D^7 ($\flat$VI^7). Work on creating smooth transitions between these changes.

At measure 7 the song moves into a pentatonic based unison riff, played by the bass and guitar, moving from the $\flat$7 (E) to the root (F#) on the 6th string, then F# to E an octave above on the D string.

A Section (Verse)

The A section starts with a repeated 16th-note rhythmic figure based over an F#^{7} and F#^{9} chord. Notice the large shifts in positions, ranging from an F#^{7} rooted on the 2nd fret (E shape barre chord) to an F#^{9} chord rooted on the 9th fret, then F#^{7} (C shape barre chord) again rooted on the 9th fret. Notice the small chord voicings which outline key intervals key intervals – this is common practice in many styles of music, especially funk, soul, and jazz. It may help to practice these large position shifts with a metronome at a slower tempo to help work on accuracy first. Practice 'locking' in with the underlying 16th rhythm with your strumming hand, to help keep you in time. At measure 15 the harmony shifts to the IV^7 chord (B^7) for two measures before returning to the F#^{7} chord at measure 18.

The A section finishes with the same descending dominant 7th chord figure from measures 5 and 6.

B Section (Break)

The B section returns to the pentatonic riff, played in unison with the bass. Take the *D.S.* at end of section of the B section, back to the sign at beginning of section A, and play until the 'fine' sign at the last measure (measure 34).

C Section (Verse)

The guitar at section B returns to the main verse rhythm figure over the F#^{7} and F#^{9} chords.

D Section (outro)

To finish the song repeats the intro riff, with the descending 7th chord figure, before ending on eighth note unison hits, $\flat$7 (E) to the tonic (F#) on beat 1 of the last measure.

Alicia Keys

SONG TITLE: IF I AIN'T GOT YOU
ALBUM: THE DIARY OF ALICIA KEYS
LABEL: J
GENRE: SOUL R&B

WRITTEN BY: ALICIA KEYS
PRODUCED BY: ALICIA KEYS

US CHART PEAK: 4

BACKGROUND INFO

'If I Ain't Got You' was released as the second single from Alicia Key's second studio album *The Diary Of Alicia Keys*. The song was inspired by the death of singer and actress Aaliyah, and the September 11 2001 attacks in New York City, as well as events in Alicia Key's life that made her ponder over the relevance of material things.

'If I Ain't Got You' reached no. 4 in the Billboard Hot 100 charts and topped the R&B Charts. The song won a Grammy Award for Best Female R&B Vocal Performance. The video for the song featured rapper and actor Method Man as Alicia Key's on-screen boyfriend.

'If I Ain't Got You' was recorded at Kampo Studios in New York City and features Steve Jordan on drums and Hugh McCracken on guitar. McCracken was a great guitarist whose work was much in demand between the 1960s and 1980s. He recorded with many artists, including Steely Dan, Mike Mainieri, Billie Joel, B.B.King, Roberta Flack, John Lennon, Paul McCartney, Idris Muhammad, James Taylor, Carly Simon, Graham Parker, Aretha Franklin, Hall and Oates, Bernard Purdie, Dr. John and Andy Gibb. He also played on Van Morrison's classic 'Brown Eyed Girl' and on Eric Carmen's 'All By Myself'. Due to the regularity of his engagements he declined joining McCartney in his new band Wings. Hugh McCracken died aged 70 in 2013.

Alicia Keys showed a promising talent at a young age. From the age of 7 she studied classical piano and aged 12 she enrolled in the Professional Performing Arts School in Manhattan. She graduated aged 16 as a valedictorian. Her piano playing and vocal delivery are testament to her considerable talent and her recognisable style blends her classical roots with the urban sounds of her youth into a singular mix of contemporary R&B and gospel.

Alicia Keys has released six studio albums to date and embarked on seven successful world tours. Her album sales are over 35 million worldwide and her single sales are in the region of 30 million. She has won 15 Grammy Awards. Alicia Keys is involved in a great deal of philanthropic activity and is a vocal critic of the objectification of women in the music and entertainment industries. In 2017 she received Amnesty International's Ambassador Of Conscience Award.

If I Ain't Got You (Live)

Alicia Keys
Words & Music by Alicia Augello Cook

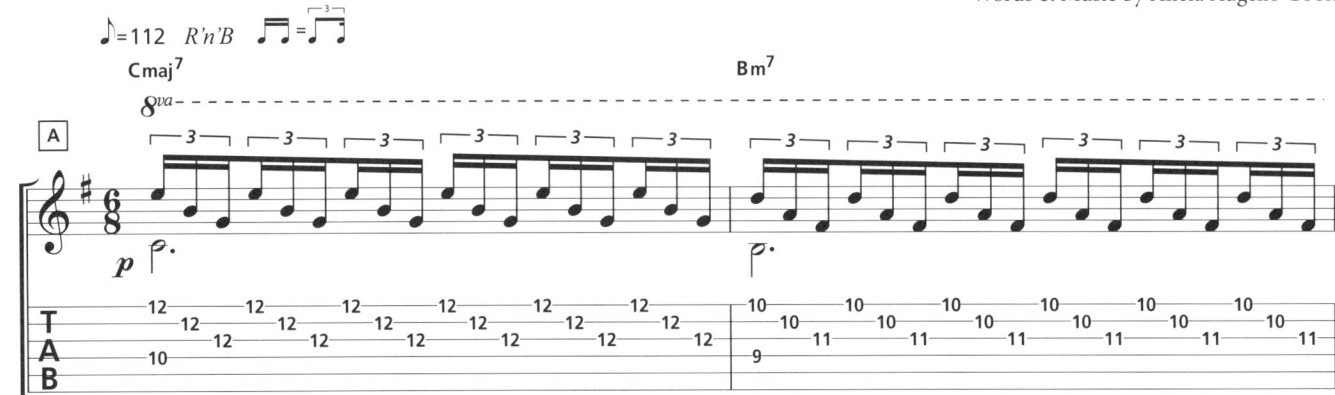
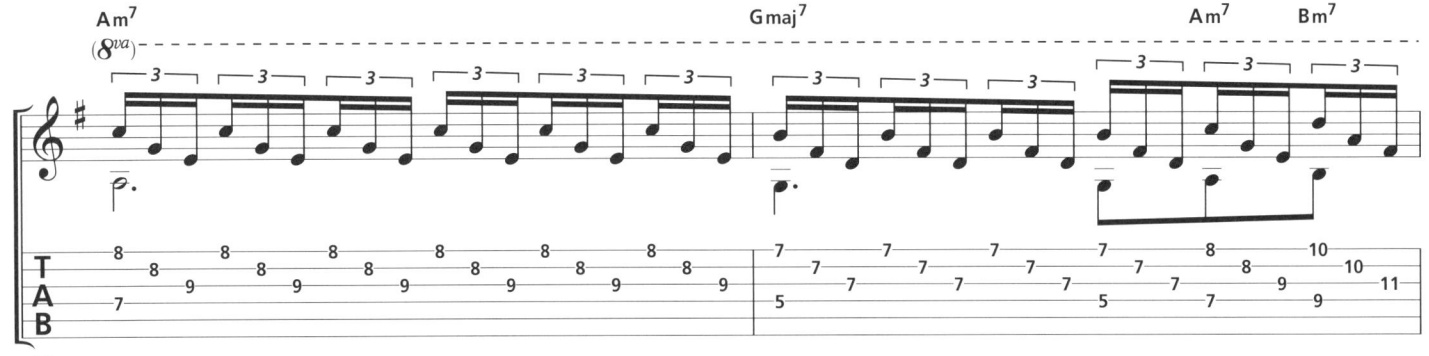
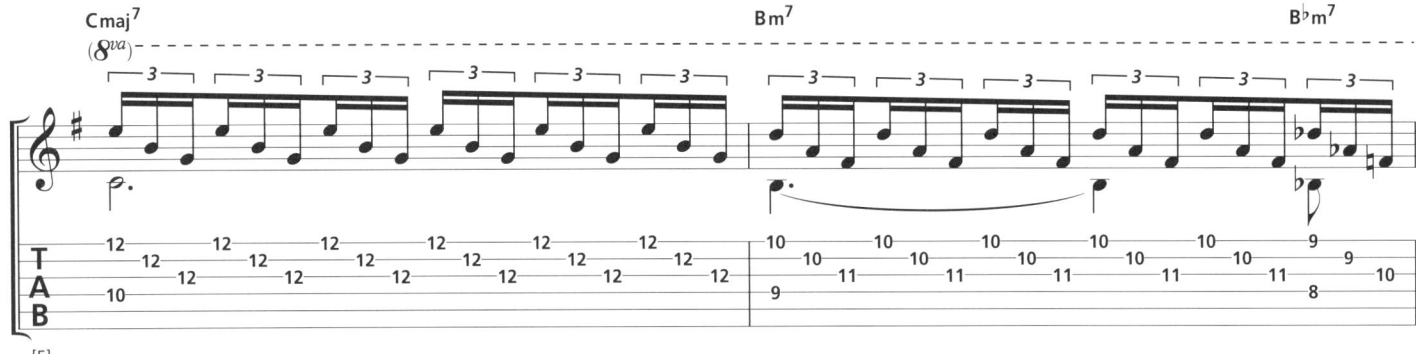
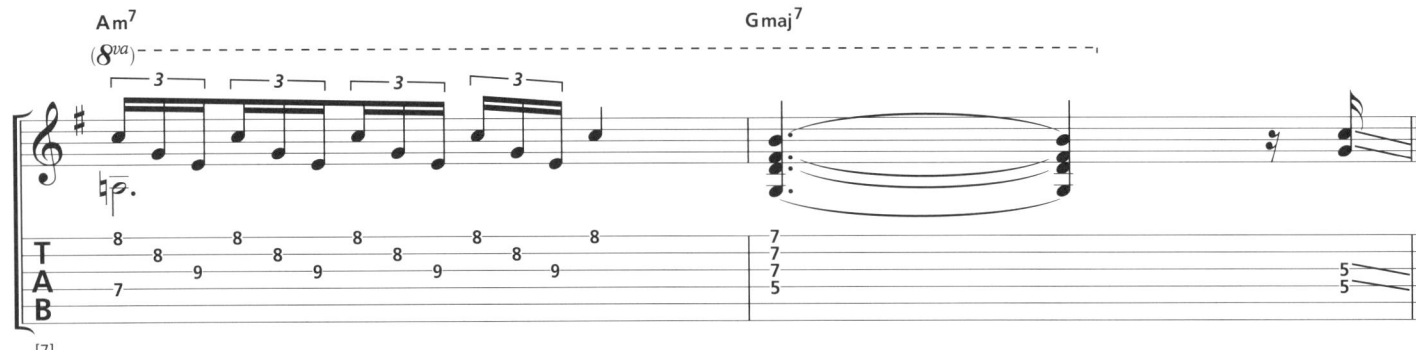
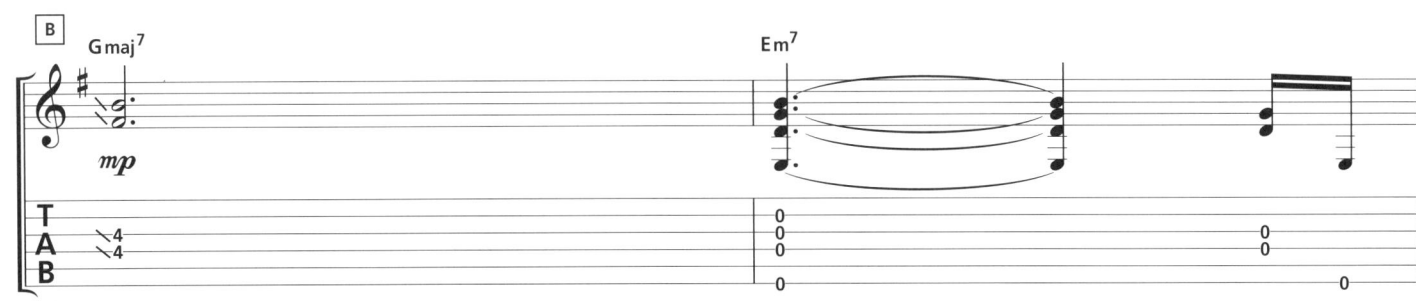

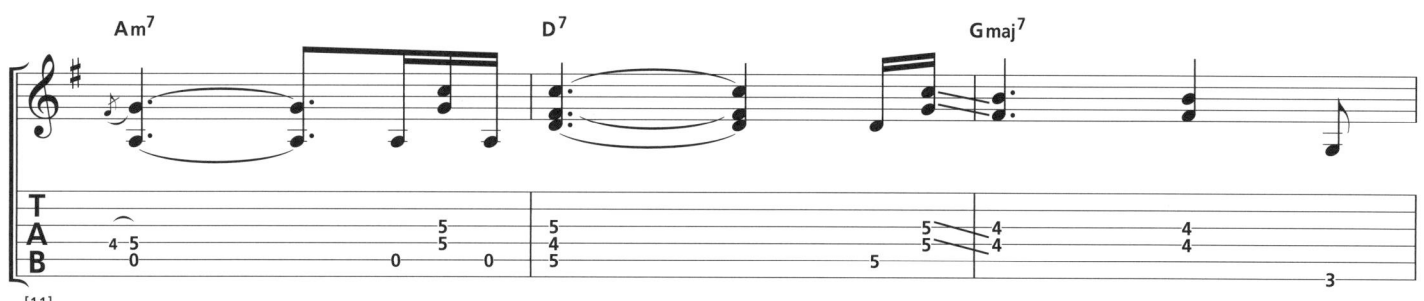
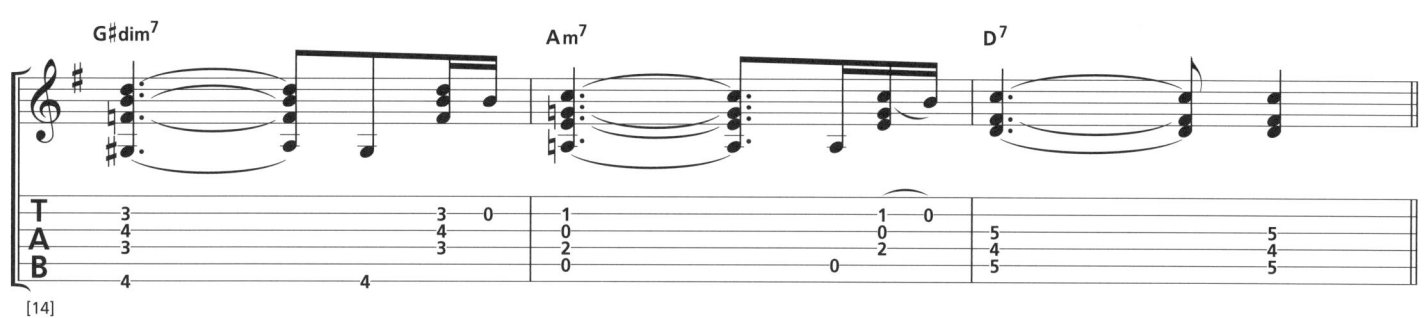
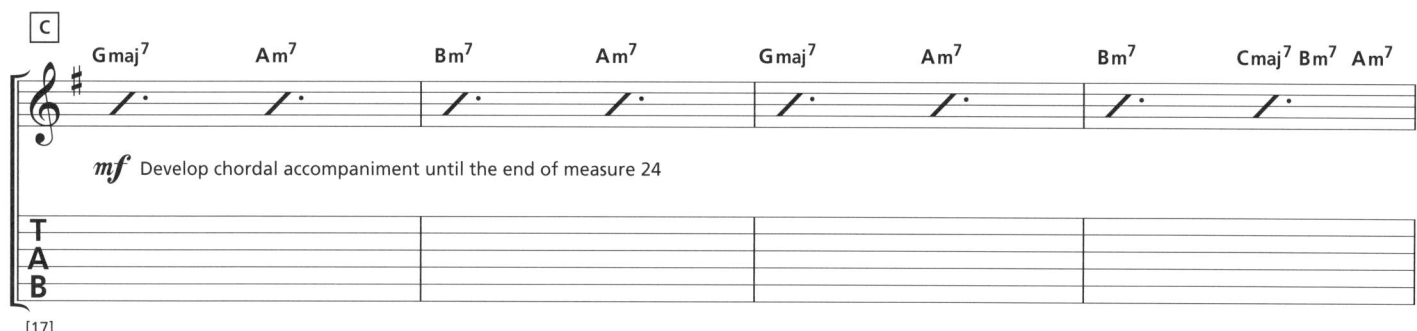

mf Develop chordal accompaniment until the end of measure 24

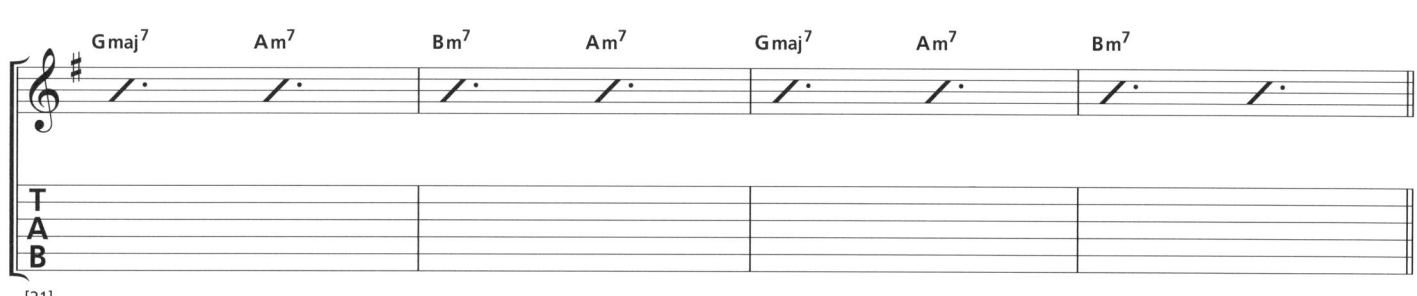
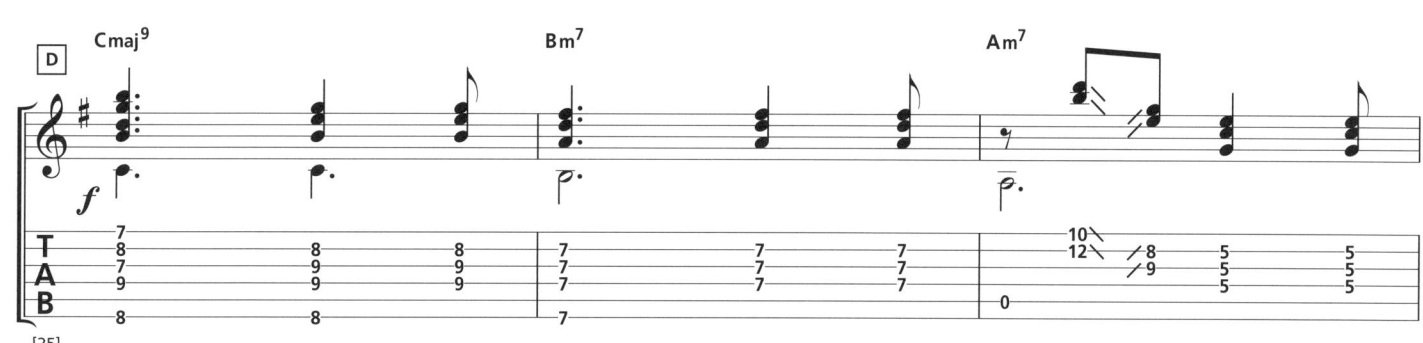

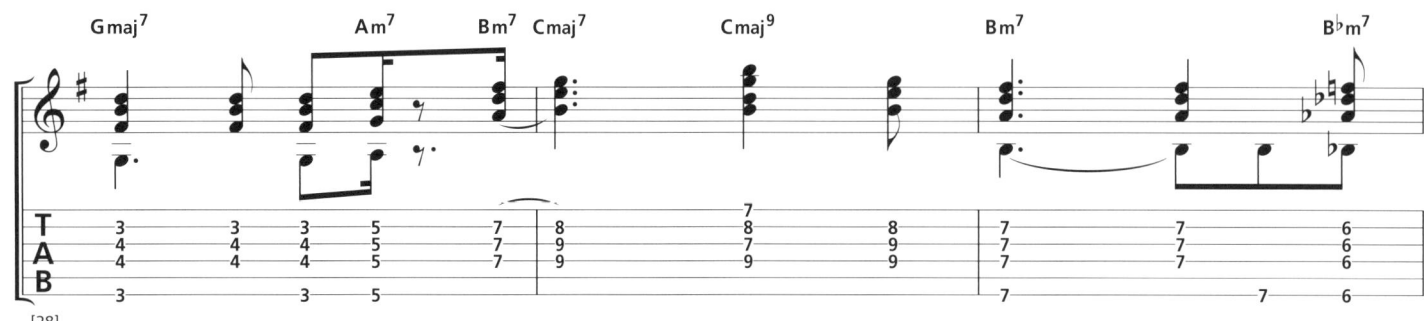
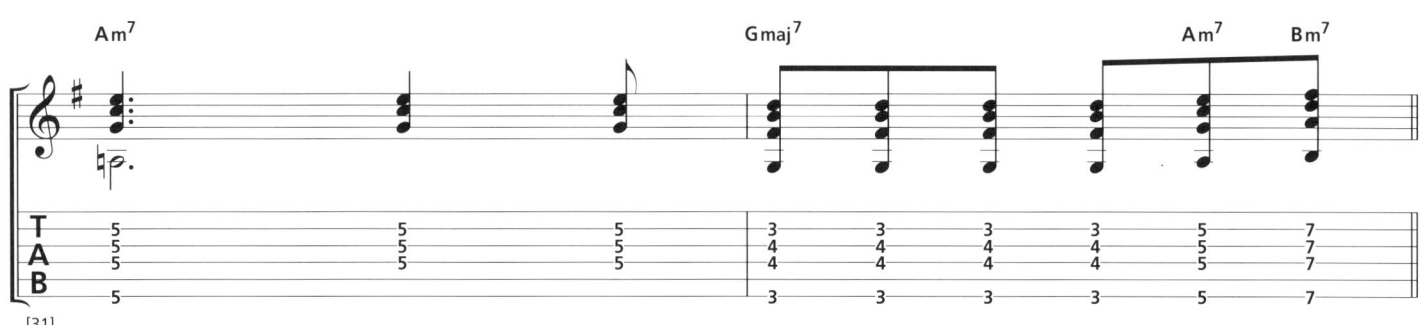
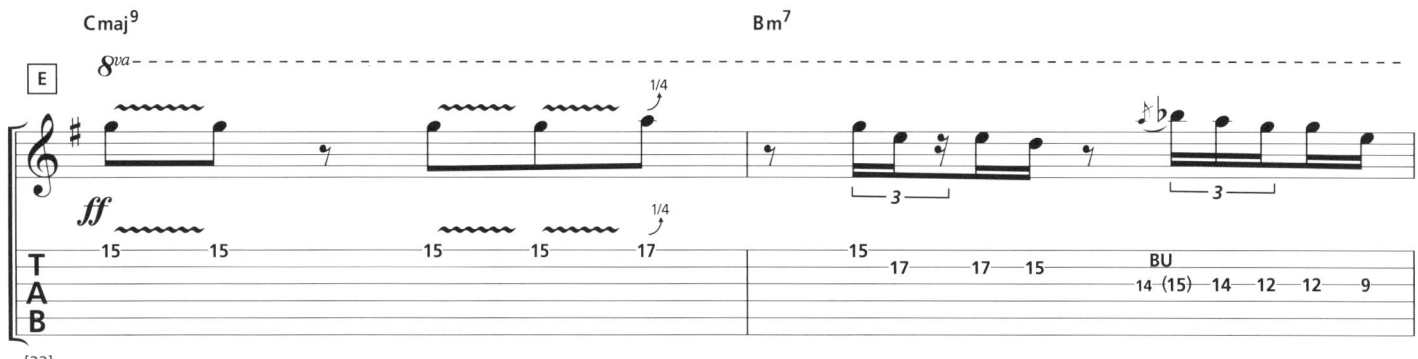
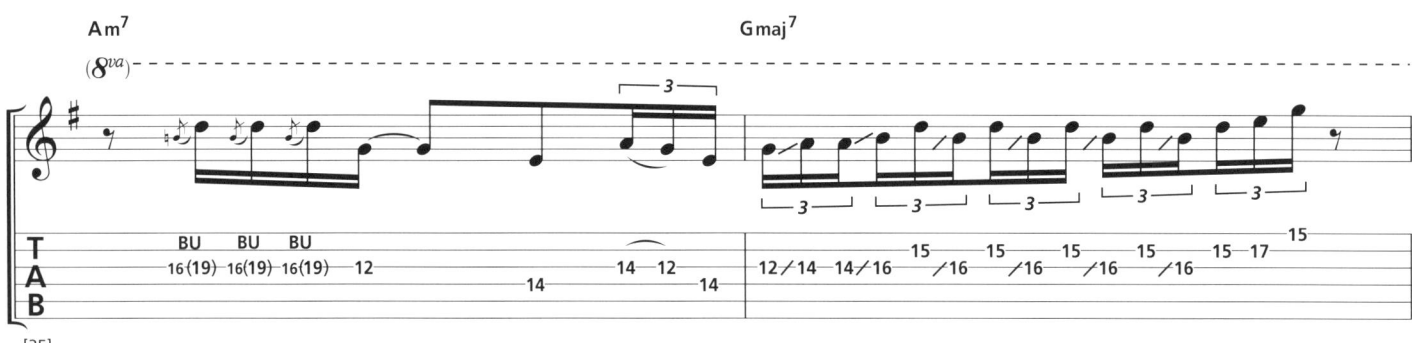
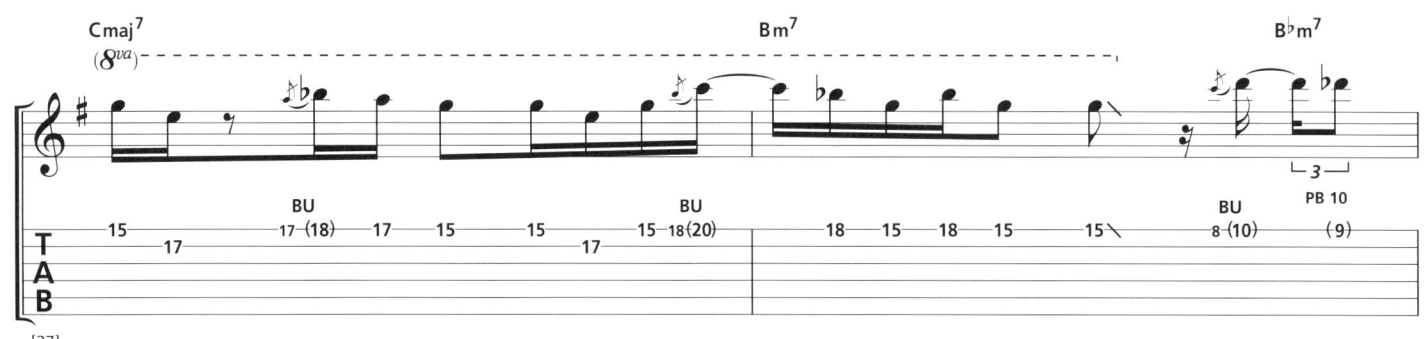

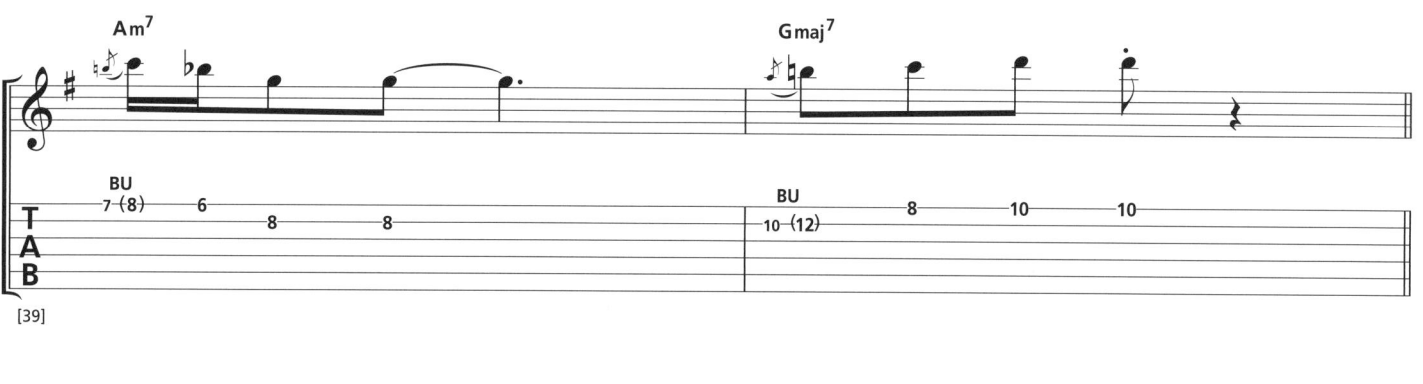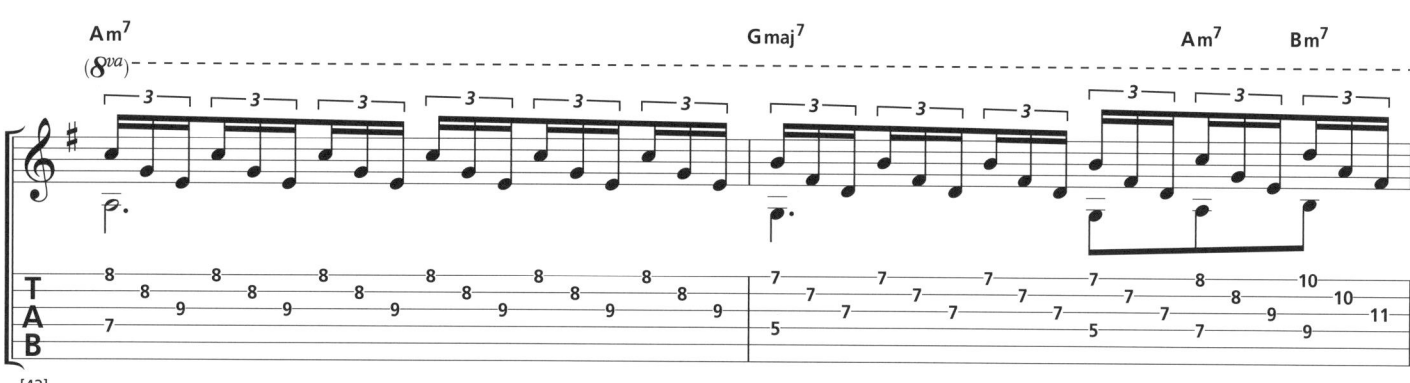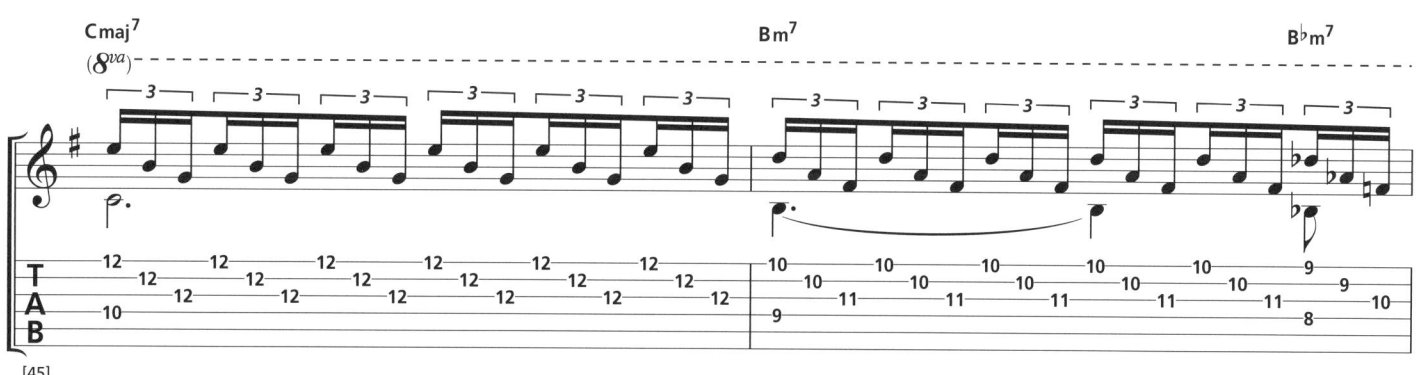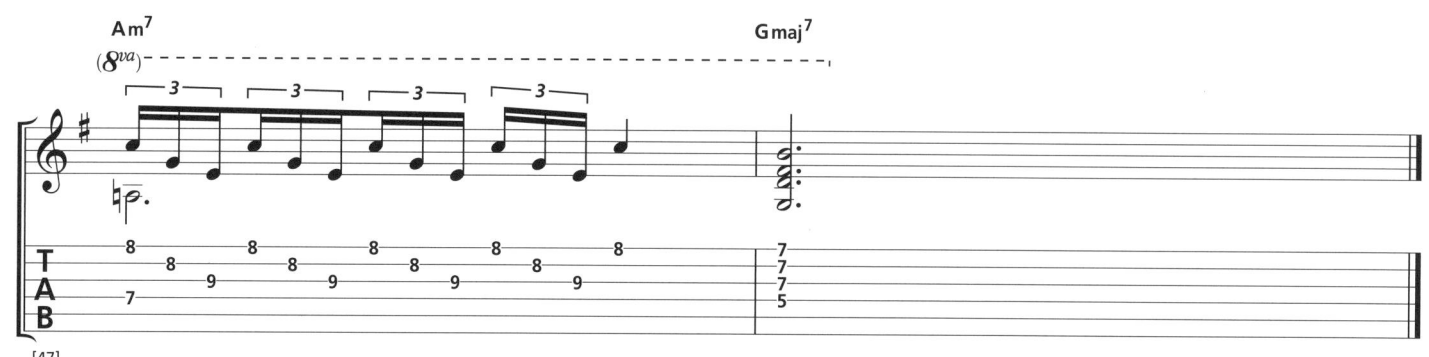

Walkthrough

Amp Settings

For the most part the guitar is replicating the piano in this guitar arrangement so a clean sound with a balanced tone is what is needed. A single coil neck pick would achieve this. The solo needs to have some edge added to the sound and a switch to bridge and middle pickup if played on a Strat based guitar or the bridge pickup on a two pickup guitar.

Piano/Rhythm Guitar:

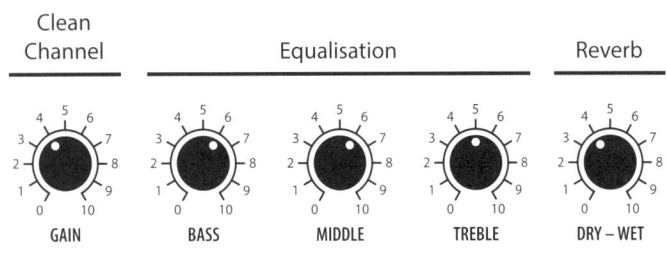

Lead Guitar:

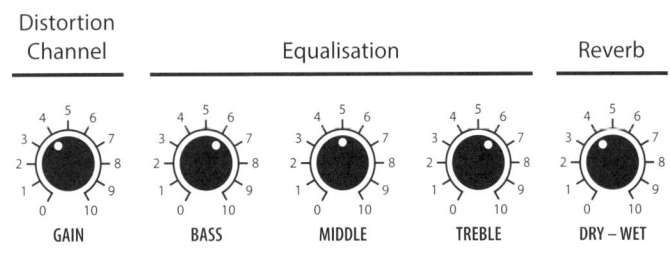

A Section (Measures 1–8)
This is the Intro section of the song and is a free flowing piano arpeggio with minimal accompaniment.

Measures 1–8 | *Finger-picked arpeggios and the 6/8 time signature*
This song is in the time signature of 6/8. This should feel like 2/4 with each beat split into a triplet. This A section sees the piano playing an arpeggio pattern through Cmaj^7, Bm^7, Am^7 and Gmaj^7. It will sound best being finger picked and it is important to get good independence with the picking hand's fingers in order to have balanced timing. The changes between the chords need to be fluent and not staccato.

B Section (Measures 9–16)
The B section is the sparse piano part in the verse of the song.

Measures 9–16
The playing is very minimal in this section providing little touches under the vocals on the original. There is a lovely use of a G#dim^7 to travel between the Gmaj^7 and Am^7 chords. Using the first finger to barre on the third fret makes this shape a little easier.

C Section (Measures 17–24)
This is the Pre-chorus section of the song.

Measures 17–24 | *Develop chordal accompaniment*
Here you can develop your own chordal accompaniment to compliment the groove. It can help to listen to live versions, and focus on voice leading between your chord voicings.

D Section (Measures 25–32)
This can be viewed as the chorus section of the song.

Measures 25–32
As this is the Chorus section the dynamic lifts and the part gets slightly busier than the Verse to fill out the overall sound. If playing with a vocalist it is important to be playing a supportive role and not be the main focus.

E Section (Measures 33–40)
This is the solo section of the song.

Measures 33–40 | *Solo*
This is a transcription of the solo that John Mayer played when he joined Alicia Keys playing this song live in Times Square in 2016. The solo is predominantly consisting of blues phrases in the G major Pentatonic. John regularly throws in the minor 3rd either played directly or as a bend to prevent the solo sounding too happy and too correct as this will detract from the blues and gospel feel. The laid back timing, dynamics, bends and vibrato are all absolutely crucial to capture the authentic feel in this section.

F Section (Measures 41–48)
This is the return to the arpeggio intro pattern for the outro of the song. The dynamic needs to drop back down and a slight rallentando at the end will help the fall into the final chord.

Jill Scott

SONG TITLE: THE REAL THING / THE WAY
ALBUM: WORDS AND SOUNDS VOL. 3 / WHO IS JILL SCOTT? WORDS AND SOUNDS VOL. 1
LABEL: HIDDEN BEACH
GENRE: NEO SOUL / R&B

WRITTEN BY: JILL SCOTT, ANDRE HARRIS, VIDAL DAVIS, JASON BOYD AND RYAN TOBY, SCOTT AND ANDRE HARRIS
PRODUCED BY: ANDRE HARRIS AND VIDAL DAVIS

US CHART PEAK: 60

BACKGROUND INFO

Jill Scott broke into the neo soul scene with her critically acclaimed debut album *Who Is Jill Scott? Words and Sounds Vol.1* The record went platinum in the US and includes the song 'The Way'. Scott's third record, *The Real Thing: Words and Sounds Vol. 3*, was also a great success and contains the song 'The Real Thing'.

Jill Scott dropped out of a career in teaching, disillusioned with the work. She always wrote poetry and started out as a spoken word artist and was discovered by Ahmir Thompson (Questlove), drummer in The Roots. She collaborated with the band in the studio and had her first live performance with them. She later collaborated with Eric Benét and Will Smith and toured Canada with a production of the musical *Rent*.

Her recording debut got her noticed and established her as a significant voice in the neo soul style. Her reputation as a strong live performer grew steadily and that is captured on the two live records she has released to date, *Experience: Jill Scott 826+* and *Live in Paris+*. Jill Scott won two Grammy awards, in 2005 and 2008 respectively, and her poetry was published by St.Martin's Press in 2005.

Jill Scott has collaborated with George Benson and Al Jarreau, Anthony Hamilton, Eve, Doug E Fresh, Dr.Dre and DJ Jazzy Jeff. In the beginning of her music career she studied acting for two years in Philadelphia. She has appeared in TV and cinema productions including *Girlfriends, Cave dwellers, Hound dog, Why Did I Get Married?, The No.1 Ladies' Detective Agency, Steel Magnolias, Fringe* and *Black Lightning*.

Jill Scott is involved in charitable work and established the Blue Babe Foundation to help young minority students pay for university fees and expenses.

Jill Scott has sold over 5 million records in the US alone. She is still performing live to great acclaim and is regarded as one of the most influential voices in the neo soul and R&B genres alongside Erykah Badu.

The Real Thing/The Way (Live)

Jill Scott
Words & Music by Jill Scott, Vidal Davis,
Maurice Toby, Jason Boyd & Andre Harris

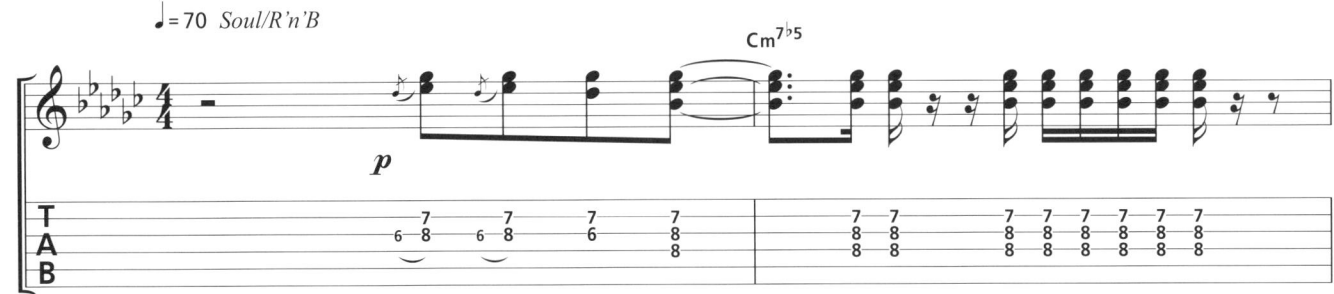

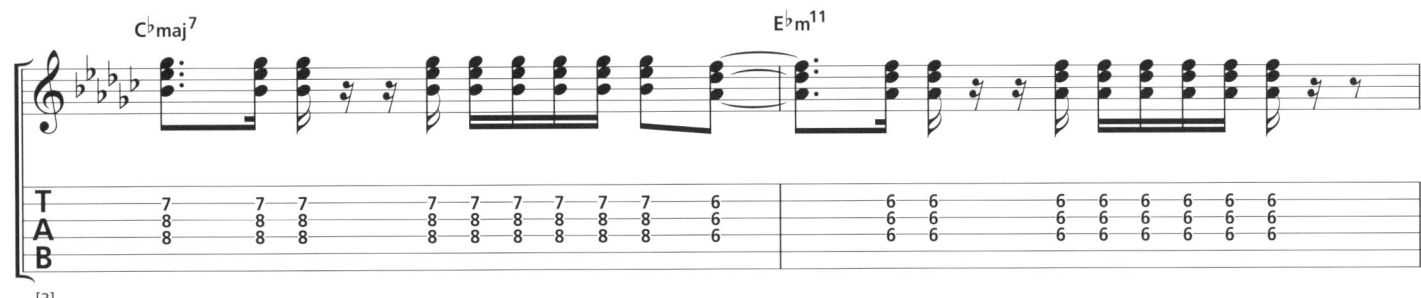

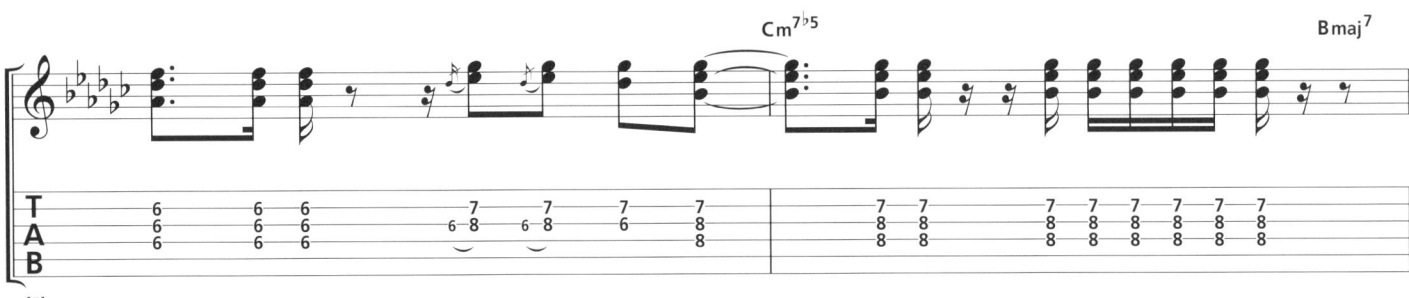

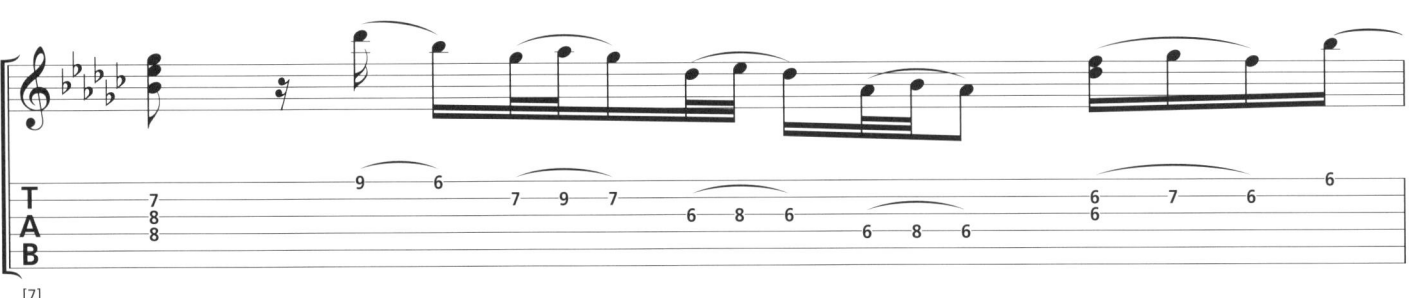

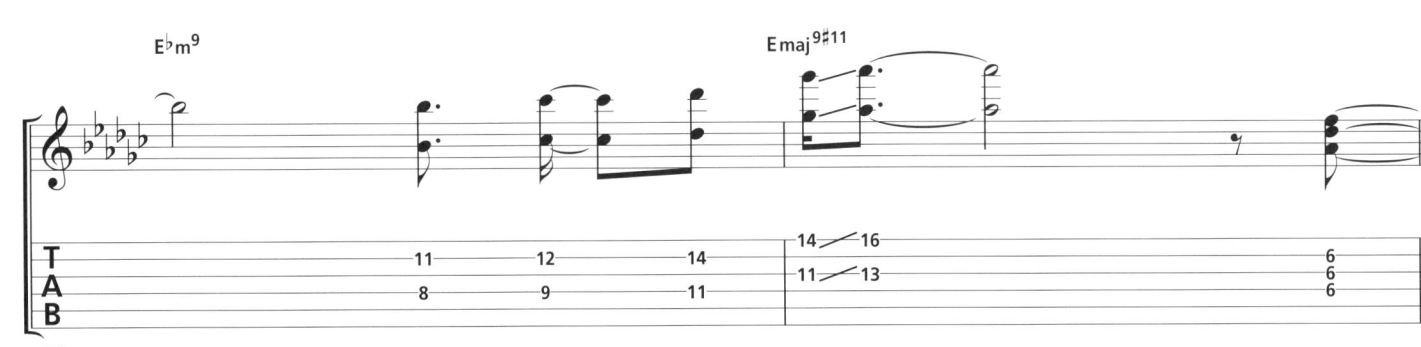

© Copyright 2007 Hitco Music/Pladis Music/Dirty Dre Music/Universal Music Corporation/EMI April Music Incorporated/Jat Cat Music Publishing Incorporated/Blue's Baby Music/Lil Vidal Music.
Universal/MCA Music Limited/EMI Music Publishing Limited/BMG Rights Management (US) LLC.
All Rights Reserved. International Copyright Secured.

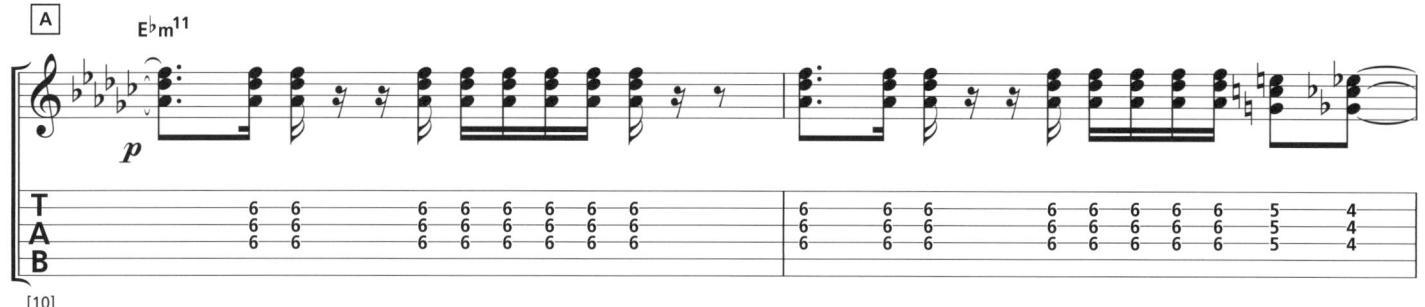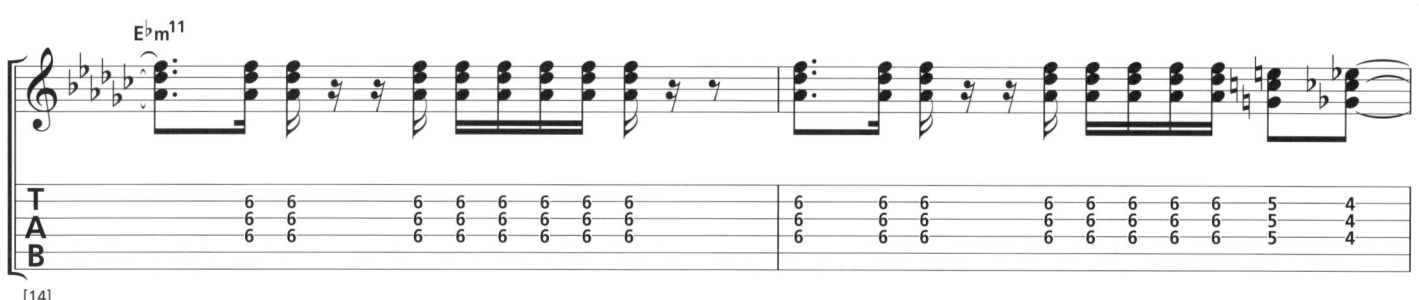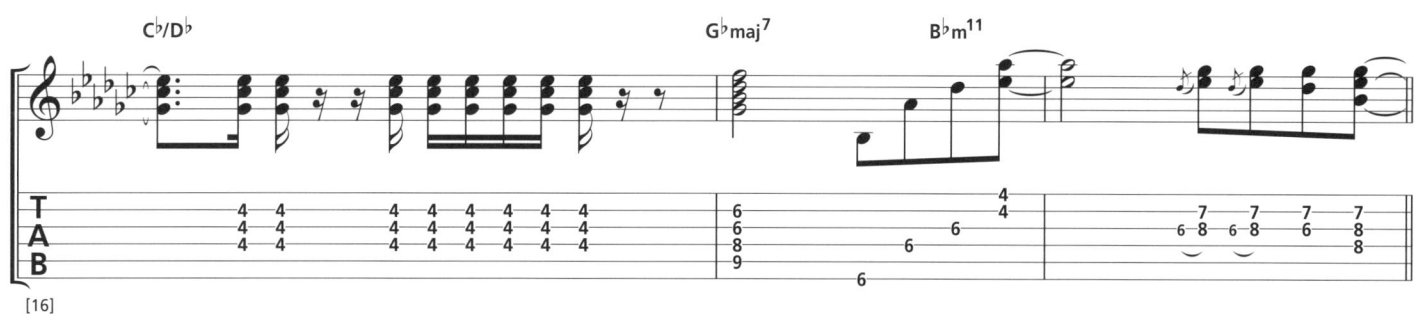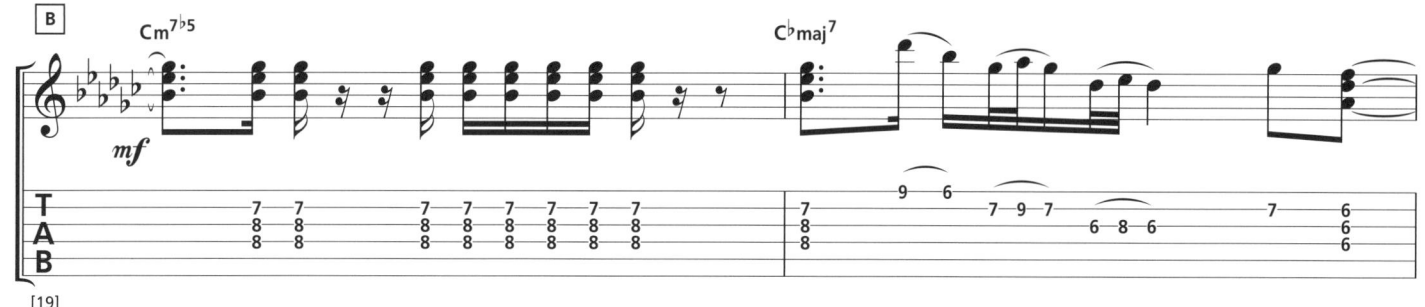

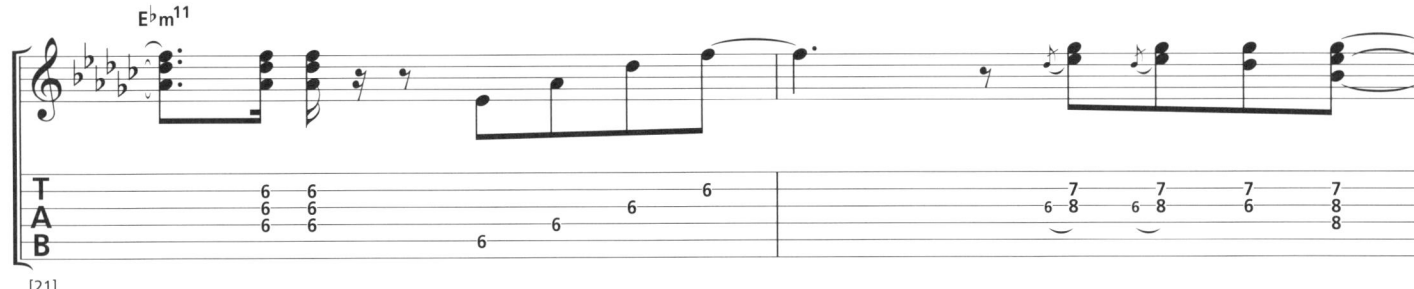
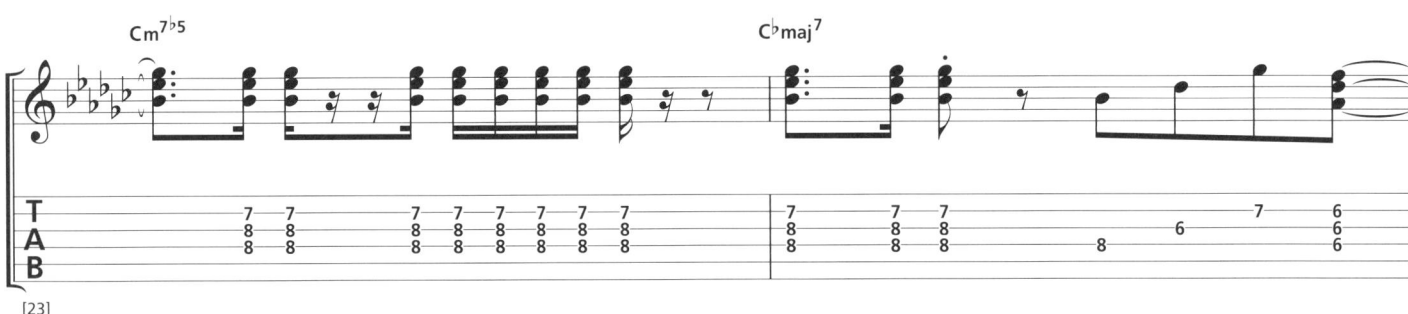
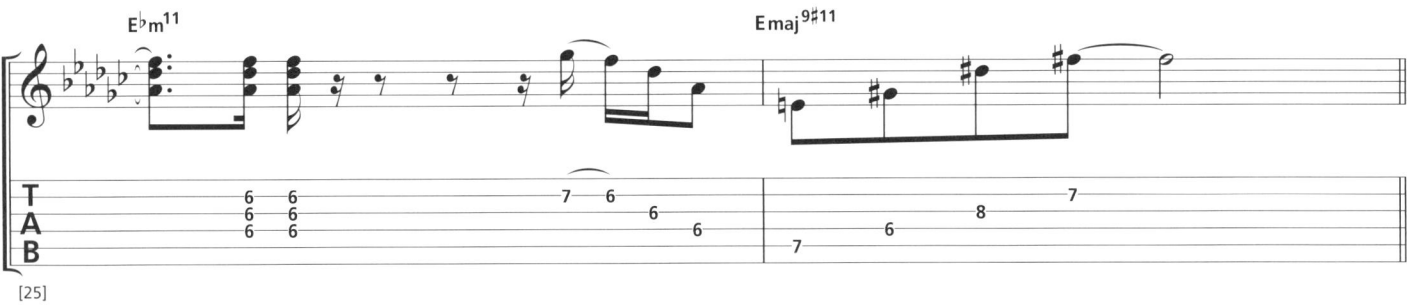

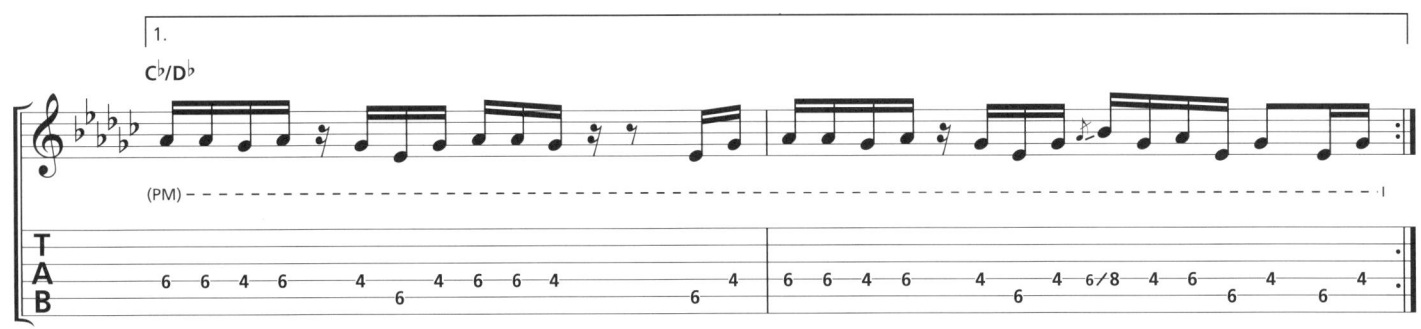

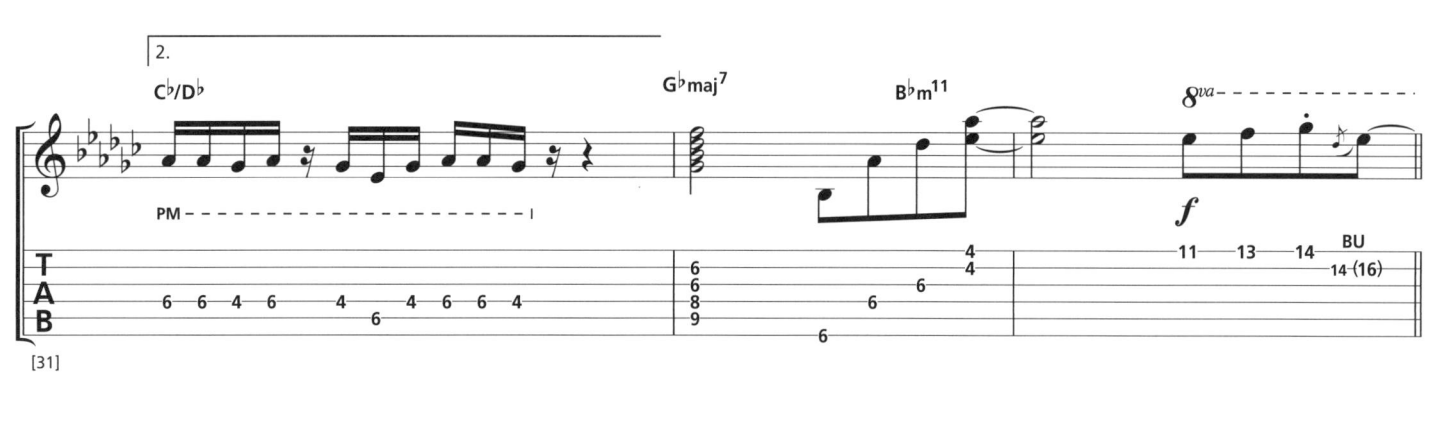
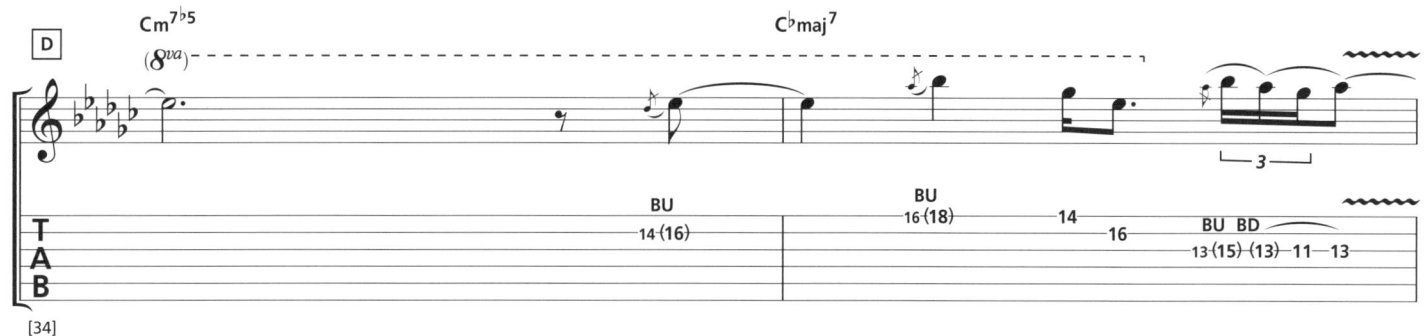
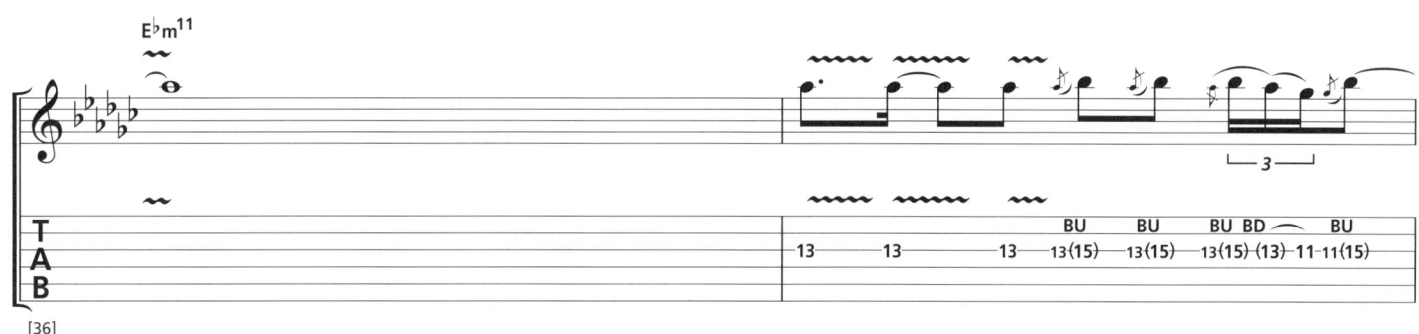
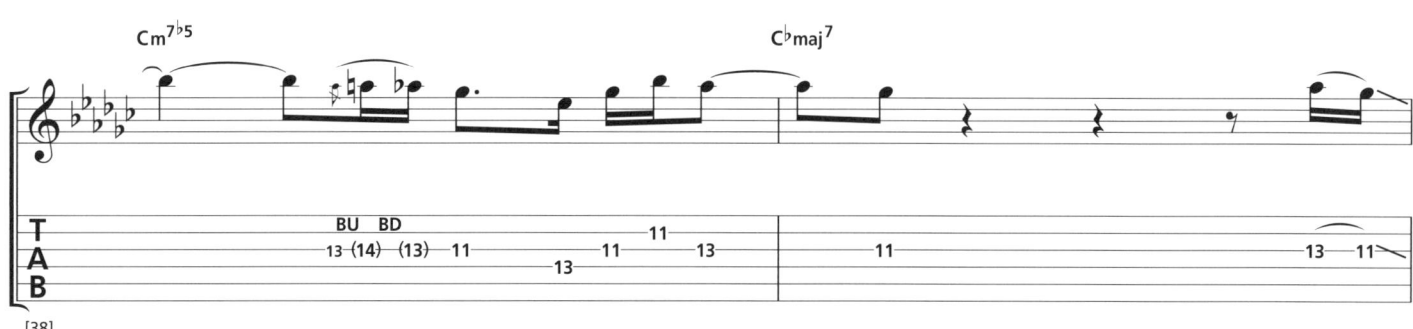
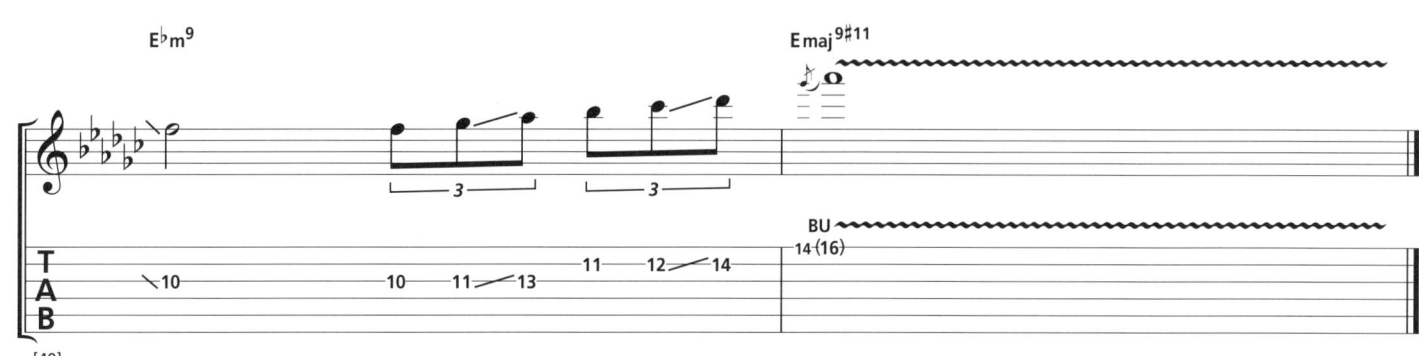

Walkthrough

Amp Settings

There are two main sounds required for this song – a 'warm' clean sound for the rhythm parts in the intro, verse and chorus, and a distorted lead sound for the solo at section D. If you are switching between the clean and dirty channels on the amp, make sure that the volume levels on both channels are set accordingly and neither channel is too loud or worse Quiet! Note that the EQ levels above are just suggestions. And depending on the guitar and amplifier you play through these settings will change. Experiment with pickup selection and tone settings on your guitar to see what different tonal colours you like and feel suit the sound of the song the best.

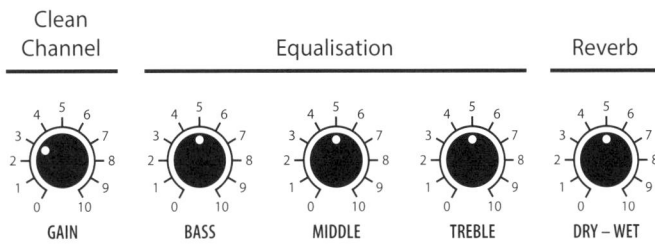

Intro

The Intro is a four measure repeated chord progression in the key of $E\flat$ minor, moving between the chords $Cm^{7\flat 5}$, $C\flat maj^7$, and $E\flat m^{11}$. The $Cm^{7\flat 5}$ has been 'borrowed' from the $E\flat$ Dorian ($B\flat$ minor parent scale), and is an example of modal interchange, which is when chords are borrowed from other scales to add variation/interest and 'colour' to chord progressions. Notice that both chord voicings of the $Cm^{7\flat 5}$ and $C\flat maj^7$ are the same ($B\flat$, $E\flat$ and $G\flat$), and it is the movement of the bass guitar from the C to $C\flat$ in measures 2 and 3 that implies the harmony has changed. In measure 7 an $E\flat$ minor pentatonic lick breaks up the chord progression before an octave line in measure 8 plays through the $E\flat$ minor scale finishing on a $Emaj^{9(\sharp 11)}$ in measure 9.

A Section (Verse)

The A section is a two chord vamp moving from an $E\flat m^{11}$ (i) to $C\flat/D\flat$ chord, which can also be seen as a $D\flat^9 sus^4$ chord ($\flat vii$). Experiment with articulation when playing the 16th-note rhythm figure. Try using a pick, but you may find that the side of your thumb will give you a subtle, consistent tone. At measure 16 the guitar plays a $G\flat maj^7$ (iii) to an arpeggiated $B\flat m^{11}$ (v) chord, to set up the B section (chorus).

B Section (Chorus)

The B section follows the same chord progression as the intro with pentatonic fills, and arpeggiated chord voicings, adding harmonic and rhythmic interest to the guitar part. Spend time becoming comfortable with the chord voicings and switching between the chordal and single note figures.

C Section (Breakdown)

The C section introduces a softer dynamic to the arrangement, where the guitar plays a single note riff over the verse changes instead of chords. The line is based on the $E\flat$ minor pentatonic scale moving between the 4th ($E\flat$), $\flat 3$ ($G\flat$), and the root note ($E\flat$).

D Section (Solo)

The solo is eight measures long, and predominantly based around the first position $E\flat$ minor pentatonic scale, playing bluesy/soulful licks over the same chords as the intro and B sections. Concentrate on intonation and vibrato during the long string bends, and the natural minor triplet line played in unison with the bass guitar in measure 40, leading to the long held bend from the $G\flat$ to $A\flat$ on the first string to finish.

Soundgarden

SONG TITLE: FELL ON BLACK DAYS
ALBUM: SUPERUNKNOWN
LABEL: A&M
GENRE: GRUNGE

WRITTEN BY: CHRIS CORNELL
PRODUCED BY: MICHAEL BEINHORN AND SOUNDGARDEN

US CHART PEAK: 54

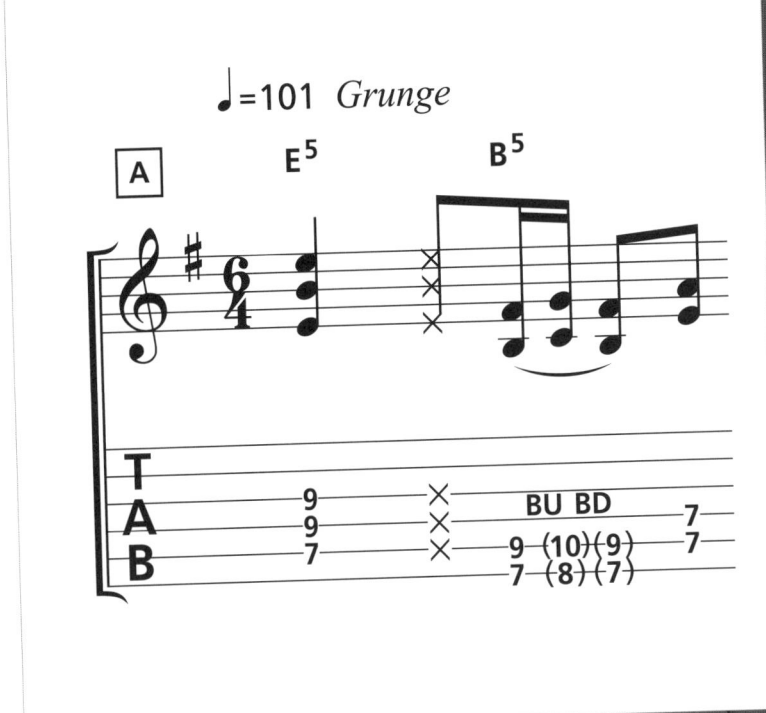

BACKGROUND INFO

Soundgarden released 'Fell On Black Days' as the fifth single from their 1994 album *Superunknown*. The record was critically acclaimed and became the band's most commercially successful album. It was certified five times platinum in the US and Soundgarden won two Grammy Awards, out of three nominations, in 1995.

Superunknown was a departure from Soundgarden's previous approach to writing. The band allowed themselves more freedom and experimentation in the creative process and more time to record each song. Lyricist, singer and main writer Chris Cornell explores dark and introspective themes, partly inspired by the work of Sylvia Plath. *Superunknown* established Soundgarden as a highly significant band that transcended their initial association with grunge and entered the realm of big league American rock bands, a path also followed by contemporaries Pearl Jam.

Soundgarden promoted *Superunknown* with extensive touring across North America, Oceania, Japan and Europe. Towards the end of the tour dates were cancelled to avoid permanent damage to Cornell's vocal chords. The recording of the follow up album signalled a further and more angular stylistic departure, moving away from riff led songs and including more acoustic instrumentation, this led to tensions in the band that would eventually become unsustainable. Soundgarden disbanded in 1997. Chris Cornell went onto form the highly successful Audioslave with Tom Morello, Tim Commerford and Brad Wilk, all former members of Rage Against The Machine, and he also released successful solo records. Drummer Matt Cameron joined Pearl Jam.

Guitarist Kim Thayil developed much of Soundgarden's sound through his heavy riffs and broad sound palette. After the band's split he worked with Pigeonhed and The Presidents Of The United States Of America. He formed the punk group The No Wto Combo, associated with the protest movement that gathered around the Seattle WTO Ministerial Conference in 1999, whose members included Jello Biafra, formerly of Dead Kennedys, Krist Novoselic, formerly of Nirvana, and Gina Mainwal from Sweet 75. Thayil also recorded on Dave Grohl's heavy metal project *Probot*. In 2003 Rolling Stone magazine named Thayil no.100 in the list of '100 greatest guitarists of all time'.

Soundgarden reunited in 2010 and recorded one studio album, *King Animal*, and toured sporadically until lead singer Chris Cornell's death in 2017.

Fell On Black Days

Soundgarden
Words & Music by Christopher Cornell

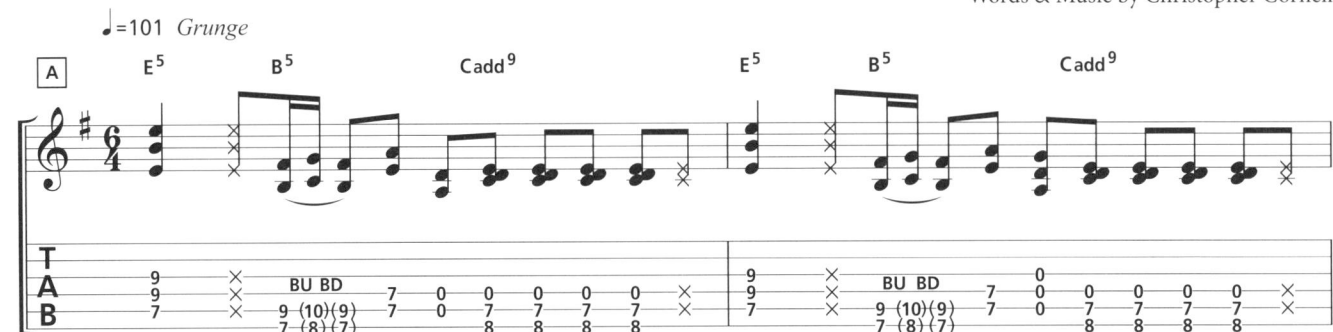
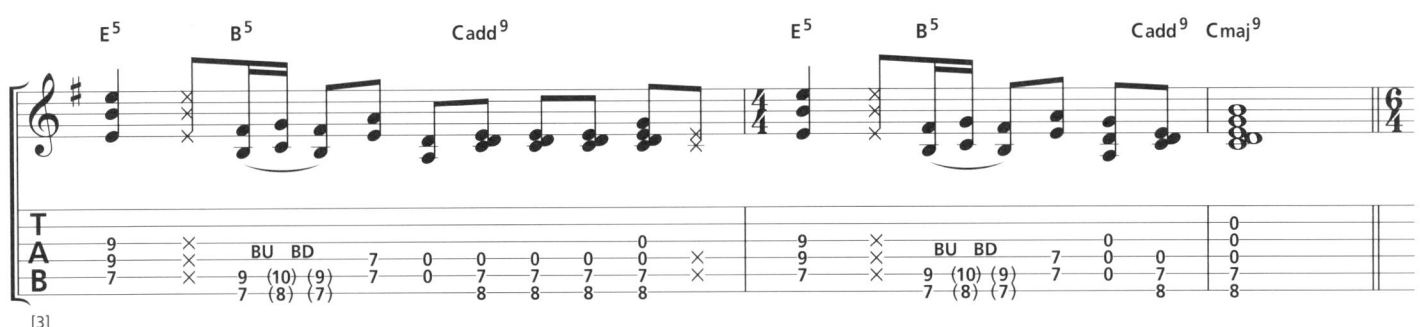
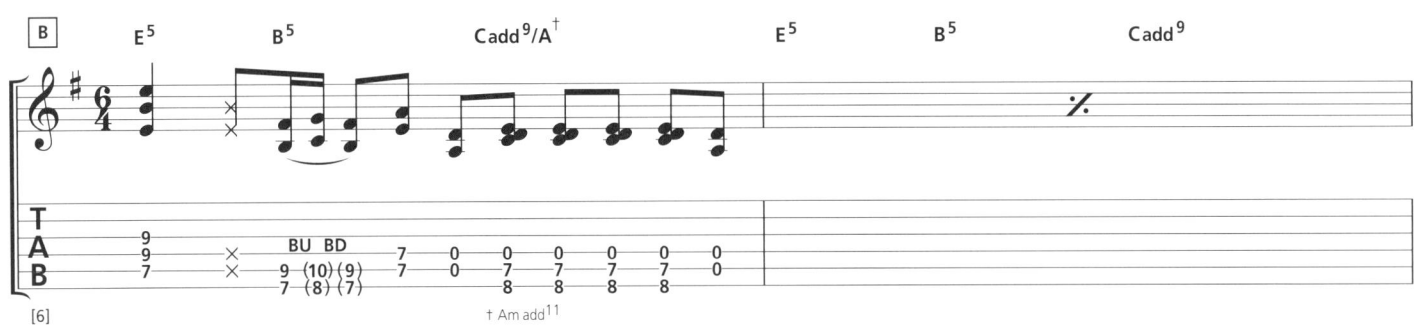
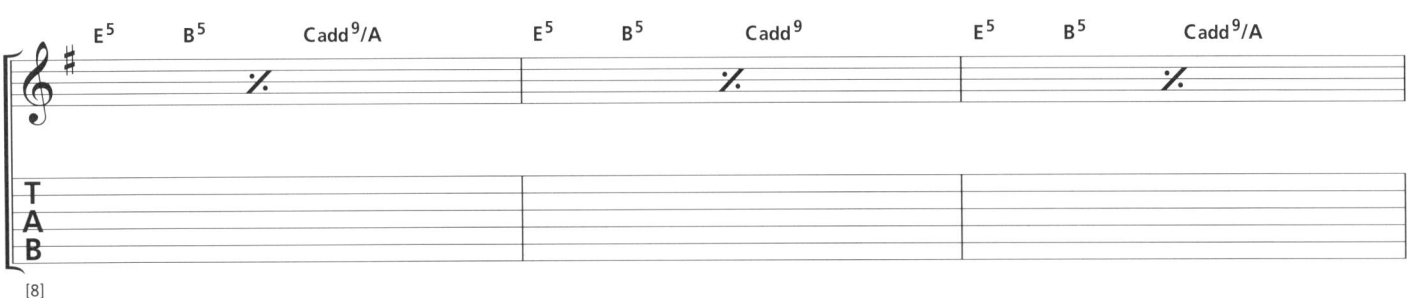
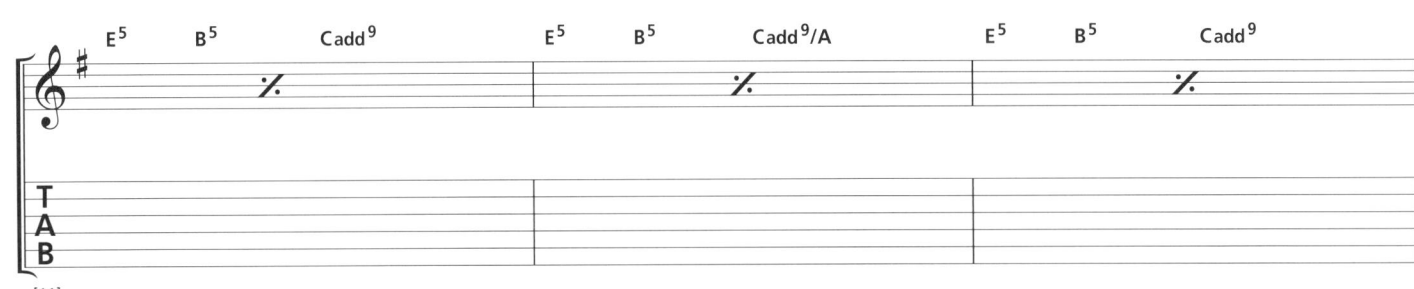

© Copyright 1994 You Make Me Sick I Make Music.
BMG Rights Management (US) LLC.
All Rights Reserved. International Copyright Secured.

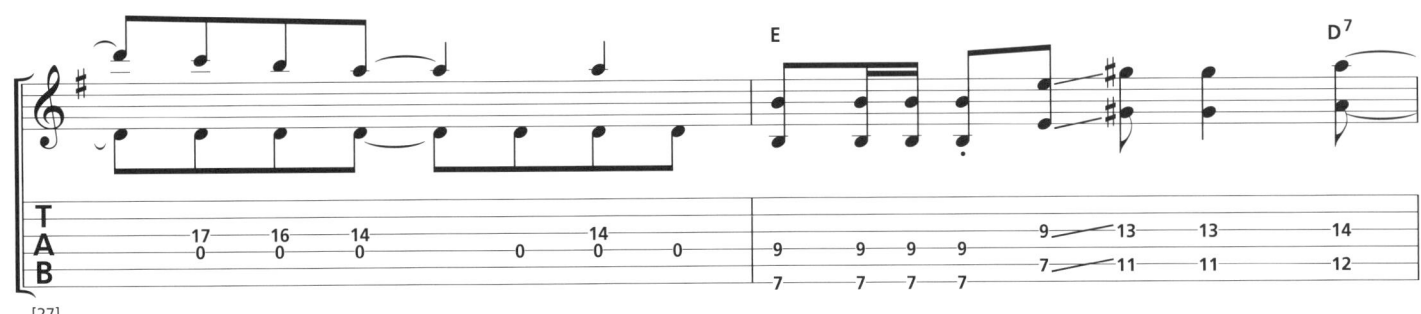

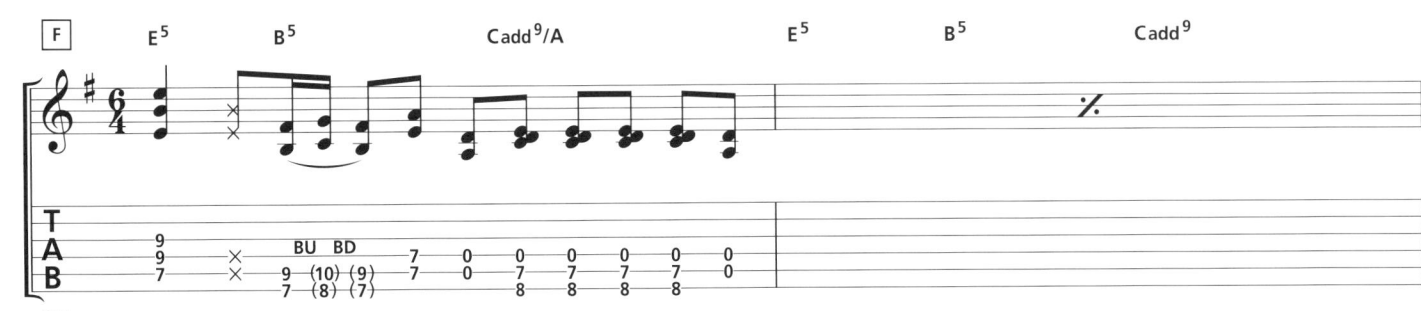

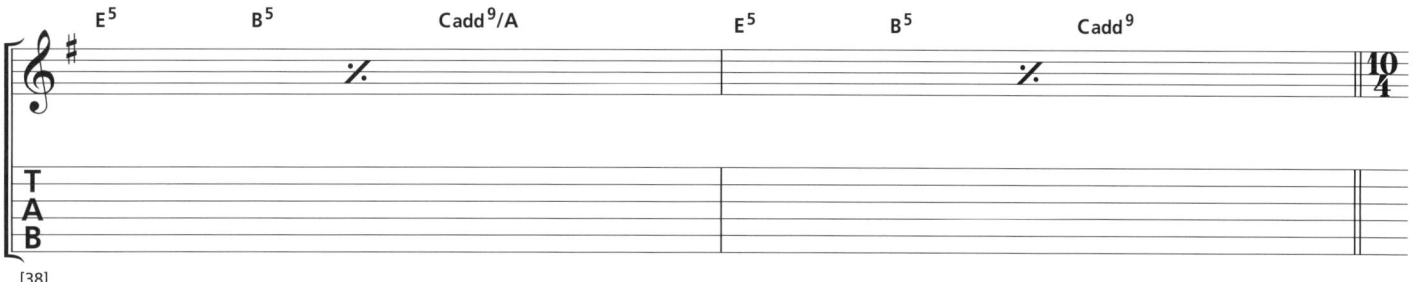
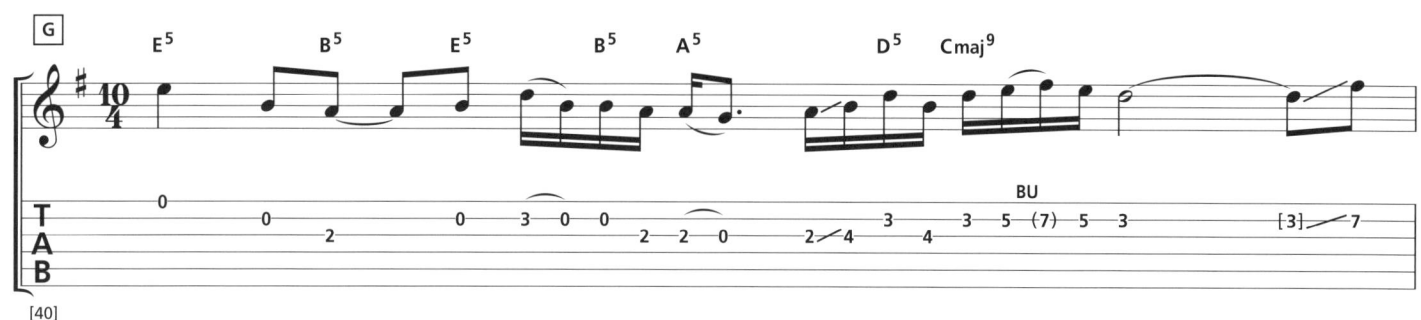
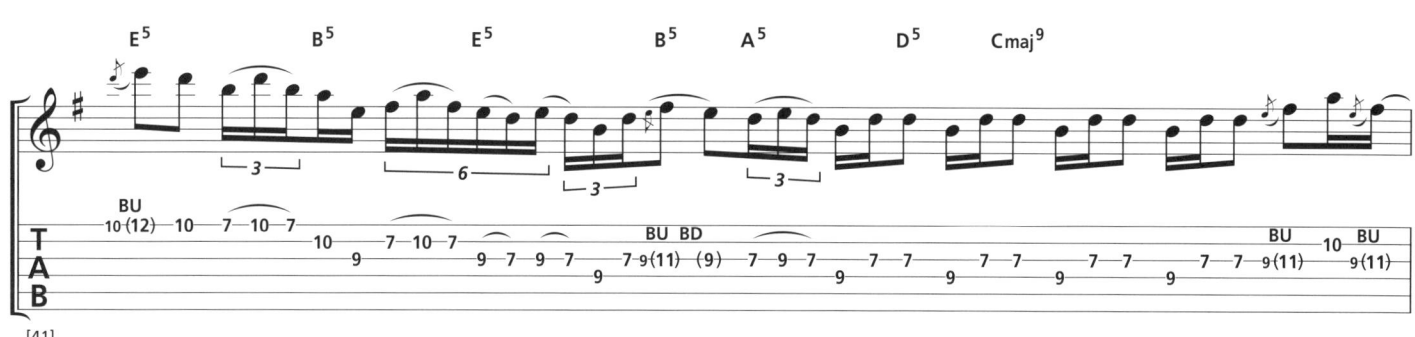
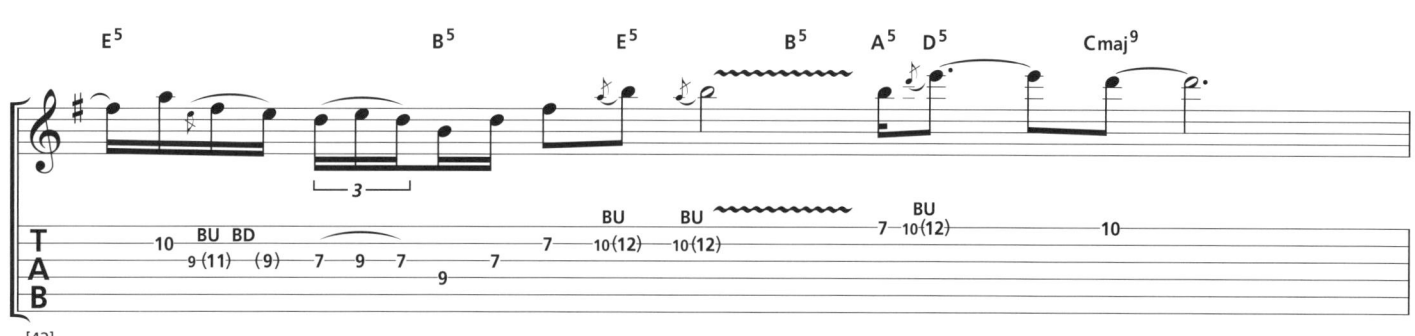
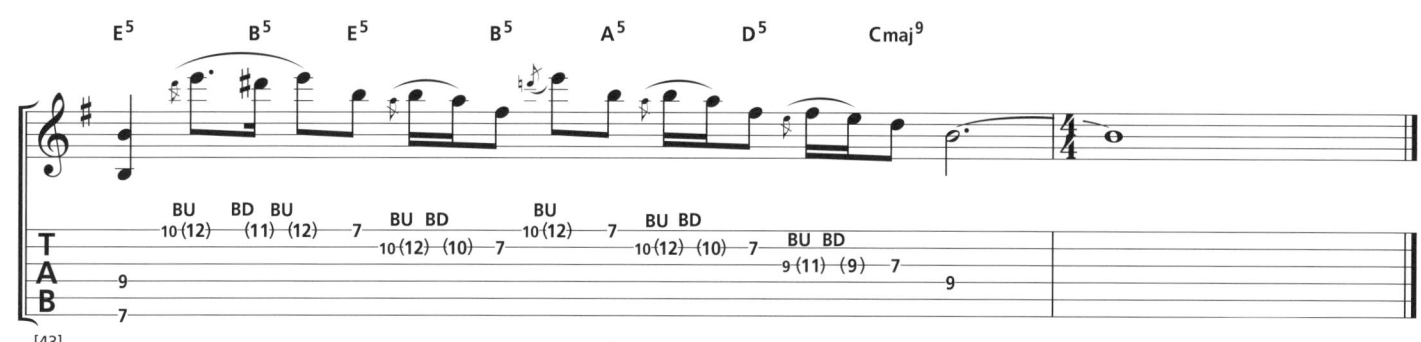

25

Walkthrough

Amp Settings

There are two guitar sounds on this track, the main rhythm part and the lead guitar. The rhythm guitar sounds as though it was recorded with a guitar with humbucker pickups, a moderate amount of distortion and a subtle room reverb. The lead guitar is overdriven more heavily, the treble is boosted, more reverb can be added and a wah pedal is used. If switching guitar sound isn't possible, using the volume pot on the guitar to roll off some volume will also decrease the amount of overdrive for the rhythm part.

Rhythm Guitar:

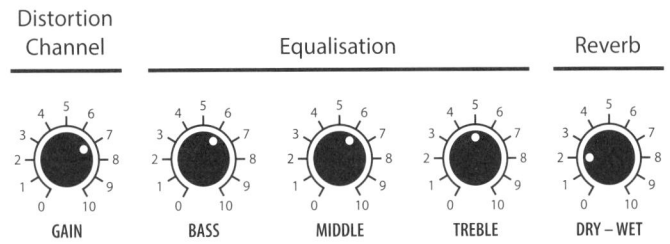

Lead Guitar:

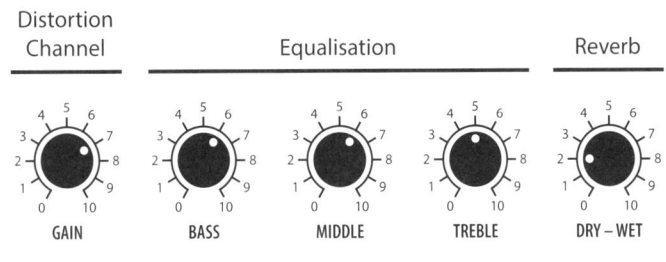

A Section (Measures 1–5)

This is the Intro of the song where the main riff is established.

Measures 1–5 | Riff and 6/4 time signature
The song is in 6/4, meaning there are 6 beats in each measure, and starts with an E^5 rooted on the fifth string, moving to a B^5 rooted on the sixth string, and is then pulled sharp to imply a C^5 chord before returning to the original pitch. In the second half of the measure the guitar is playing a C on the bottom string with the major 3rd (E) on the fifth string and an open D on the fourth string that implies a $Cadd^9$ chord. The last two measures switch to 4/4 and then it returns to 6/4 in the B section.

B Section (Measures 6–16)

This is the Verse section of the song that predominantly continues the riff established in the A section.
The riff changes in measure 15 to a riff using the E^5, B^5, A^5 and D^5 playing mainly on the off beats to give it a syncopated feel and moving into measure 16 playing a $Cmaj^9$ chord. This is the same bottom three strings as the $Cadd^9$ but adding the open G, B and E creates a major 9 with the addition of the 7th the note B.

C Section (Measures 17–20)

This is the Chorus section of the song and is the same as the main riff that was played in the A and B sections.

D Section (Measures 21–24)

The D section is a slight variation of the main riff that serves as a link into the Bridge.

E Section (Measures 25–35)

This is the Bridge section of the song that features an interesting octave and drone string pattern.

Measures 25–35 | Octaves and drone strings
The chords implied in this section are E and D^7. Over the E chord the guitar plays octaves on B, E and G♯ the 5th, Root and 3rd of the chord. The fretting hand has to be effective at muting so all strings can be strummed but only the two chosen notes heard. Over the D^7 the guitar plays a D Mixolydian line keeping the open D string droning underneath the more fiddly part on the third string.

F Section (Measures 36–39)

This is a return to the Chorus and almost a repeat of the C Section.

G Section (Measures 40–44)

This is the solo section of the song.

Measures 40–44 | Solo and the 10/4 time signature
The solo can be approached in 5/4, but it takes 10 beats for the pattern and emphasis point to line up and repeat so it may be better to think of it in 10/4. The first measure is predominantly E minor pentatonic with one bend to a major 2nd on beat 7. Measure 41 sees Kim play licks that could be viewed as B minor pentatonic which when played over an E result in the intervals Root, 2nd, 4th, 5th and ♭7th. This is the quickest measure employing many triplet 16ths. Throughout the solo he uses the wah pedal, sometimes frenetically sweeping as fast as he can and other times leaving it at the brightest point.

Prince

SONG TITLE: I WANNA BE YOUR LOVER
ALBUM: PRINCE
LABEL: WARNER BROS.
GENRE: FUNK

WRITTEN BY: PRINCE
PRODUCED BY: PRINCE

US CHART PEAK: 11

BACKGROUND INFO

'I Wanna Be Your Lover' was the lead single from Prince's eponymous second album. It was Prince's first major hit single in the US, topping the Billboard Hot Soul Singles charts and reaching the no.11 spot on the Billboard Hot 100. The song was written after Warner Bros. requested a follow up to his debut album *For You*, which underperformed commercially. 'I Wanna Be Your Lover' is a funk song delivered in falsetto throughout and describing Prince's feelings of love and frustration for a woman who considers him a child. The woman in question is pianist and singer Patrice Rushen, who wrote the highly successful 'Forget Me Nots'. Prince included a sample of 'I Wanna Be Your Lover' in his 1992 single 'My Name Is Prince'.

Prince Rogers Nelson was an astonishing young talent. He wrote his first song aged 7 and signed his first record contract aged 17. *Prince* went platinum in the US and along with Prince's first five records it blends funk, rock and dance music with explicit lyrics. His 1984 release *Purple Rain*, the soundtrack to his film debut, was a massive worldwide success selling over 20 million copies. Prince's backing band, *The Revolution*, was a highly regarded outfit with exceptional musicians in its ranks.

Prince disbanded The Revolution in 1986 and released four solo albums, including *Sign O' the Times* in 1987.

Following a contractual dispute with Warner Bros., Prince changed his name to an unpronounceable symbol, known as the love symbol. He released five studio albums between 1994 and 1996 in order to speed up his contractual obligation and move labels. Prince signed to Arista Records in 1998 and released sixteen albums. His last record was *Hit 'n' Run Phase Two*, released in December 2015. He died aged 57 in April 2016.

Prince was a phenomenal musician – a multi-instrumentalist and engineer of the highest order who often played all instruments on his recordings. He was also a consummate performer who was backed by some of the most highly respected session musicians in the business. His achievements as a writer went beyond his own record production. He wrote 'Manic Monday' for The Bangles and the worldwide success 'Nothing Compares 2 U', covered by Sinead O'Connor. He also wrote 'With This Tear' for Celine Dion and 'U' for Paula Abdul.

I Wanna Be Your Lover

Prince
Words & Music by Prince Rogers Nelson

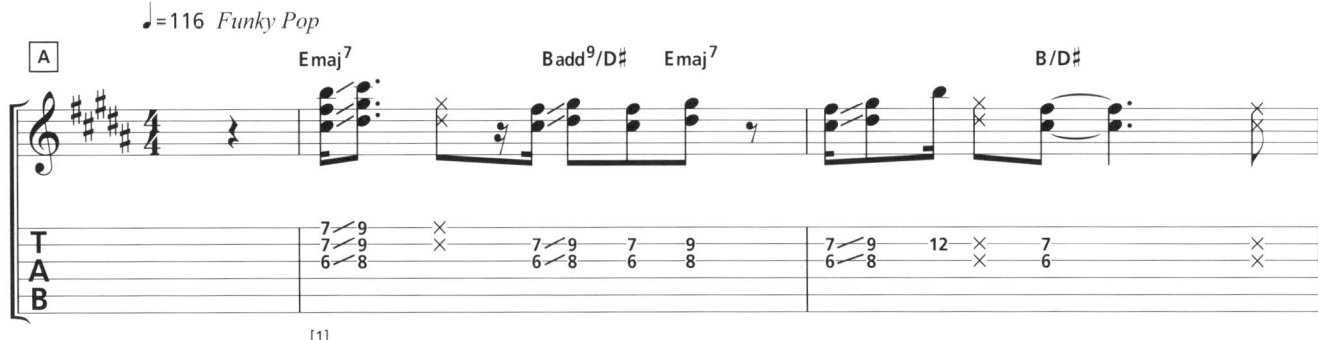

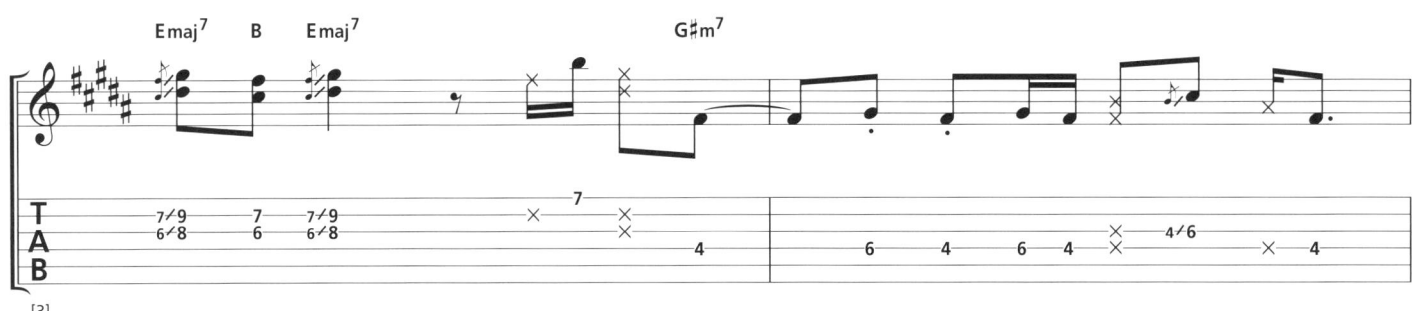

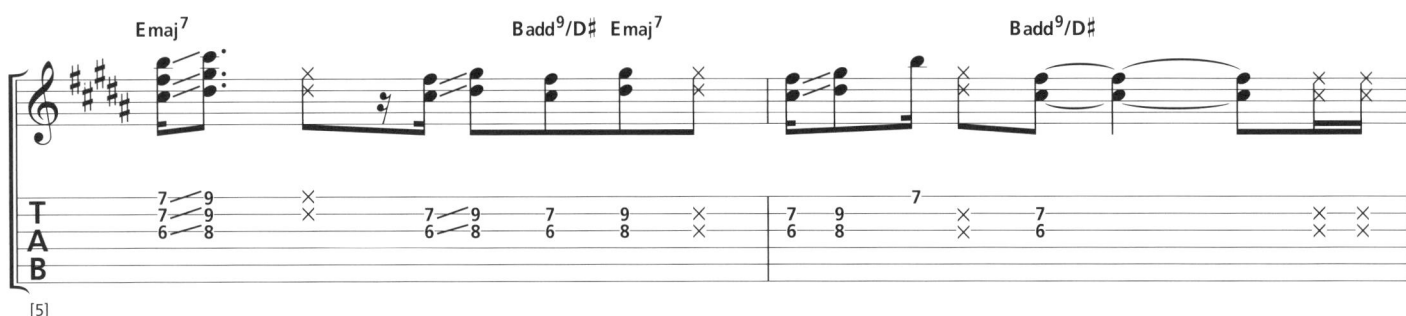

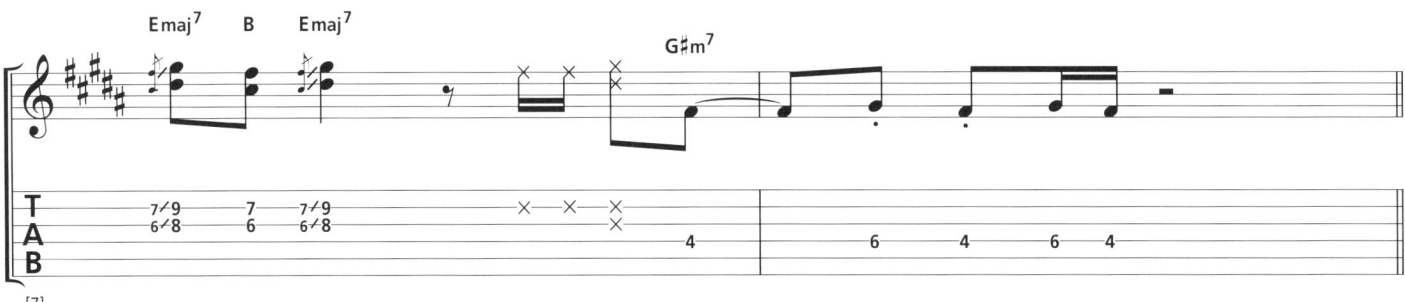

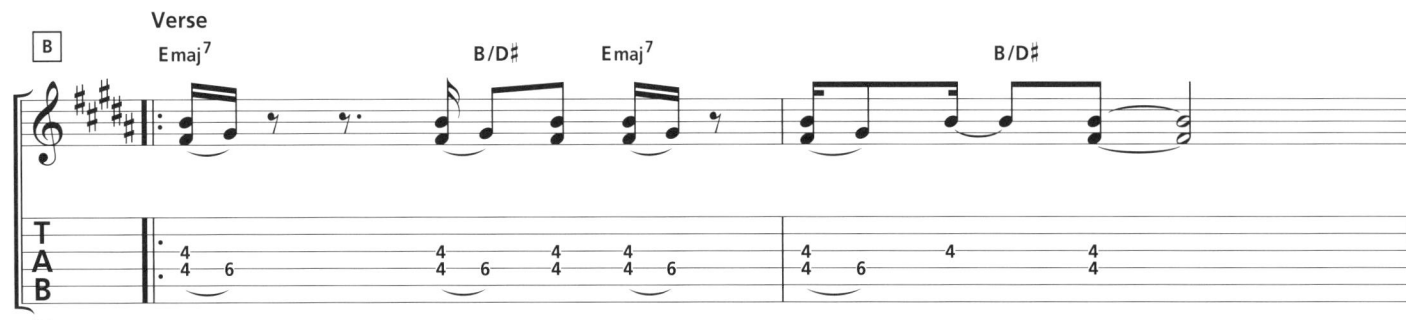

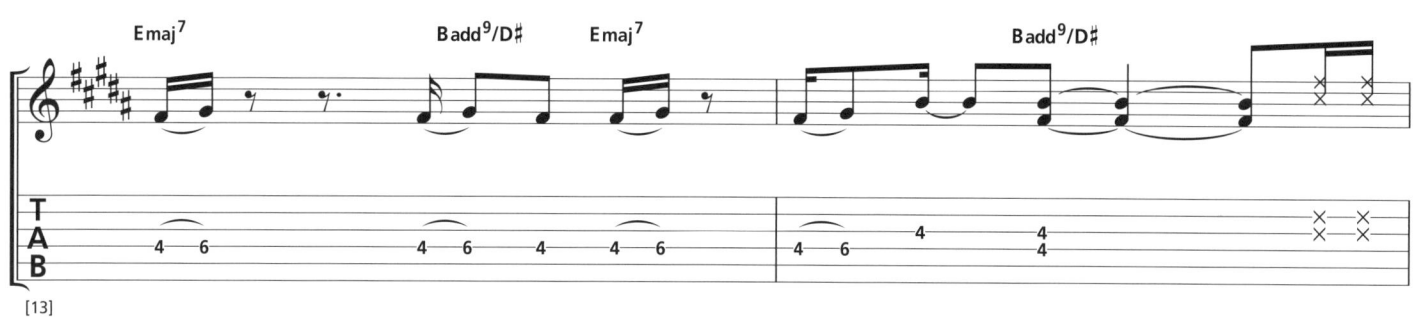
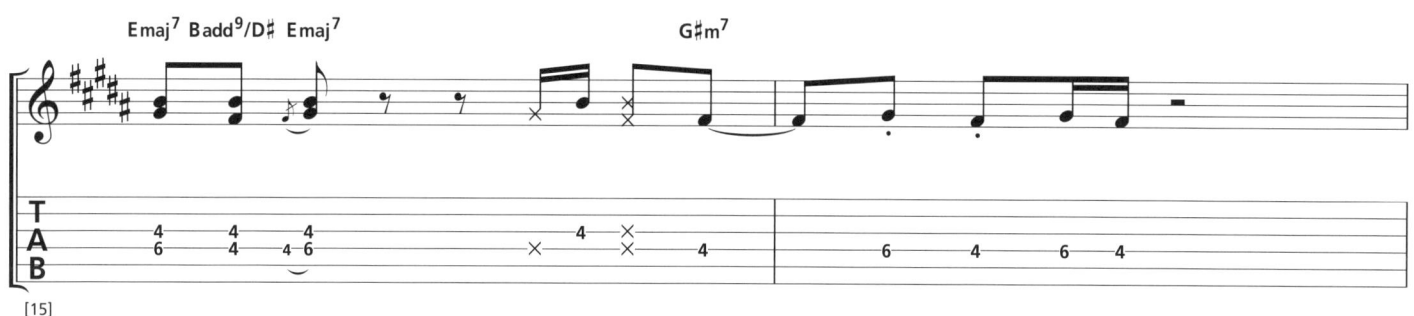
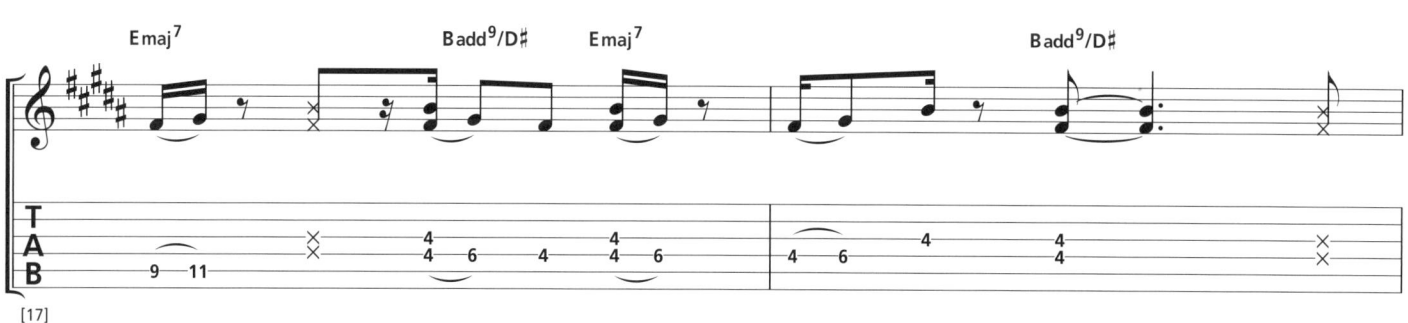
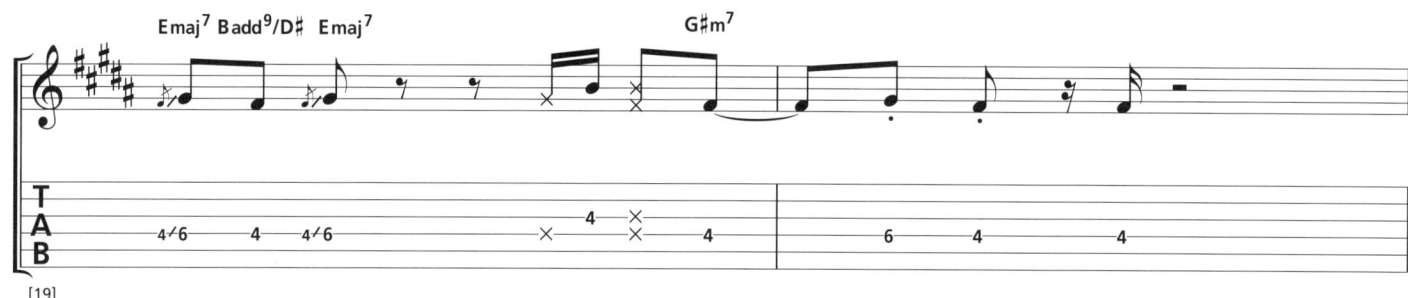

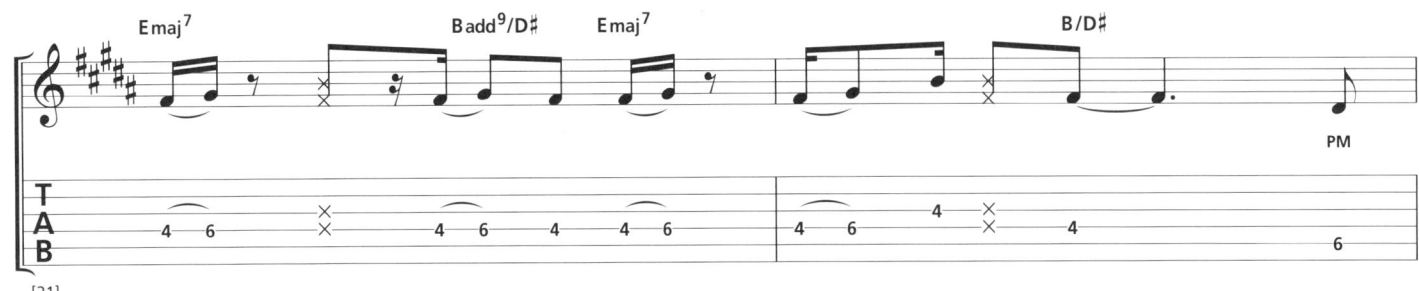
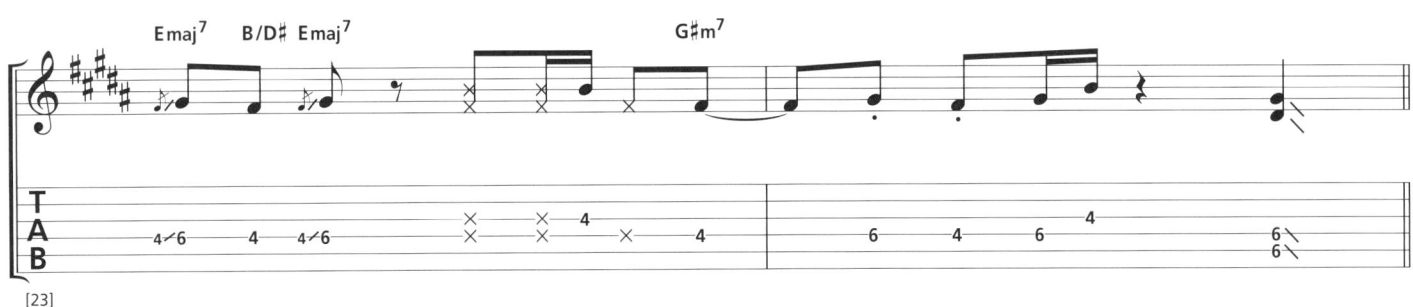
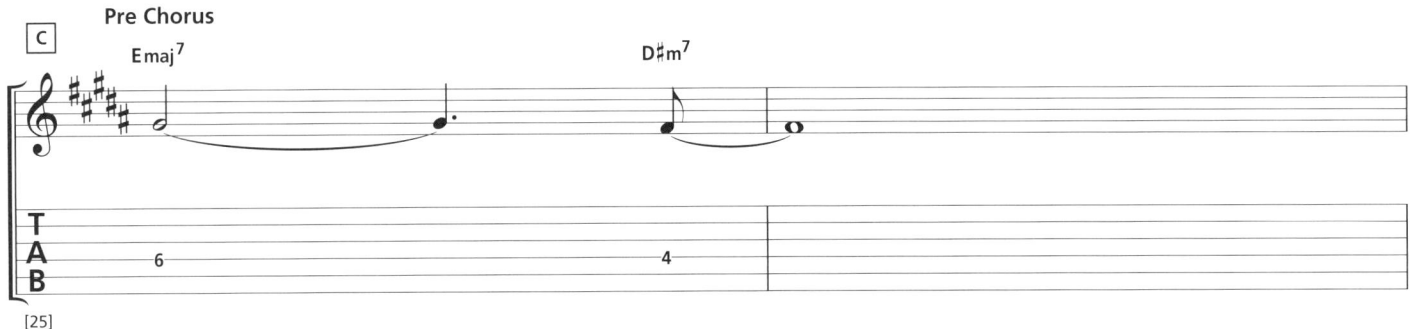
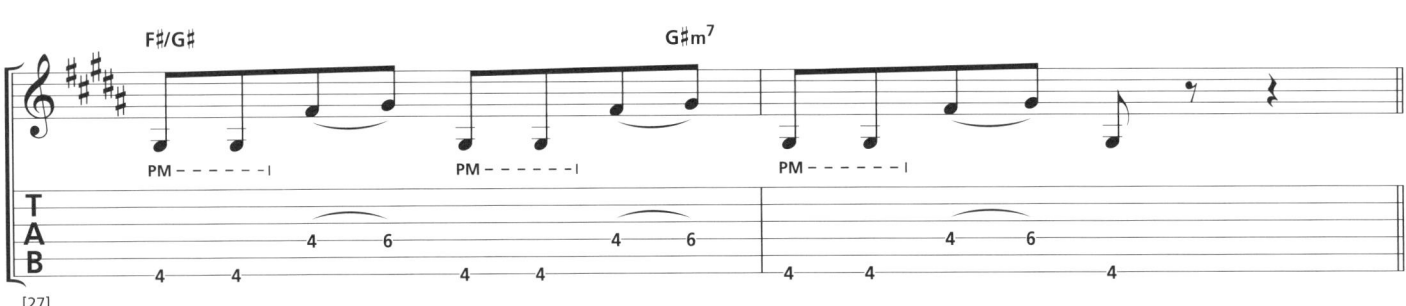
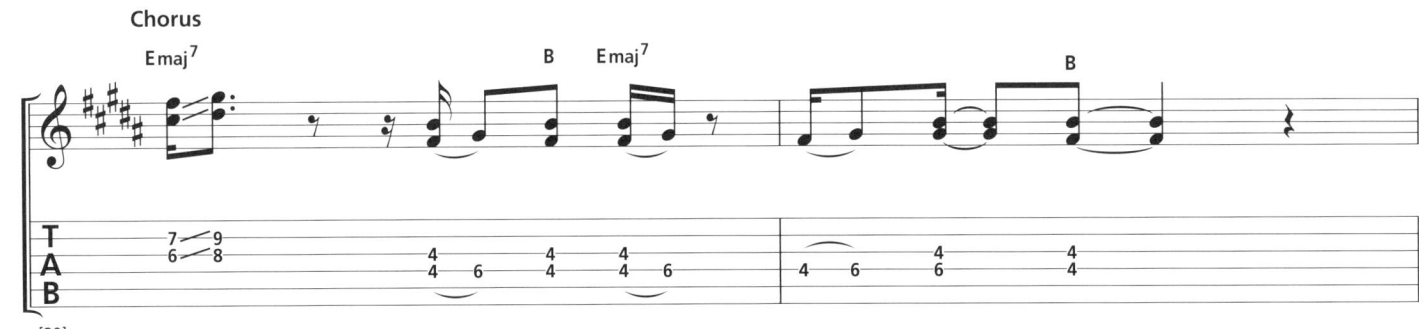

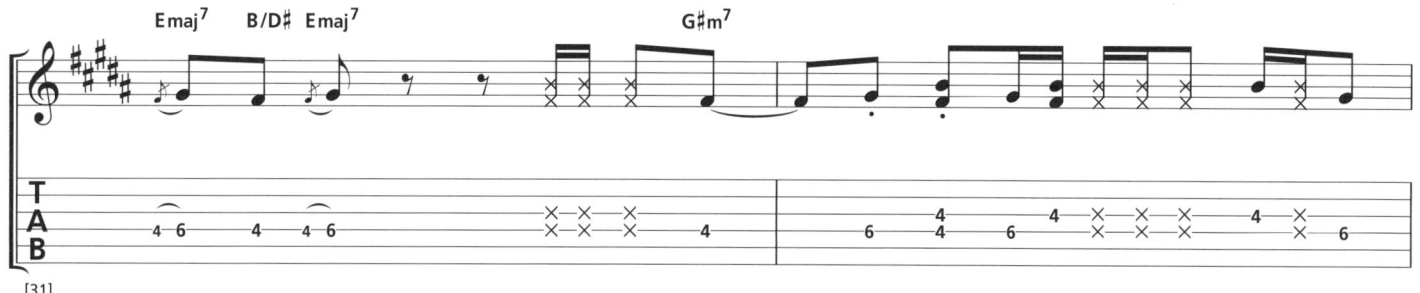
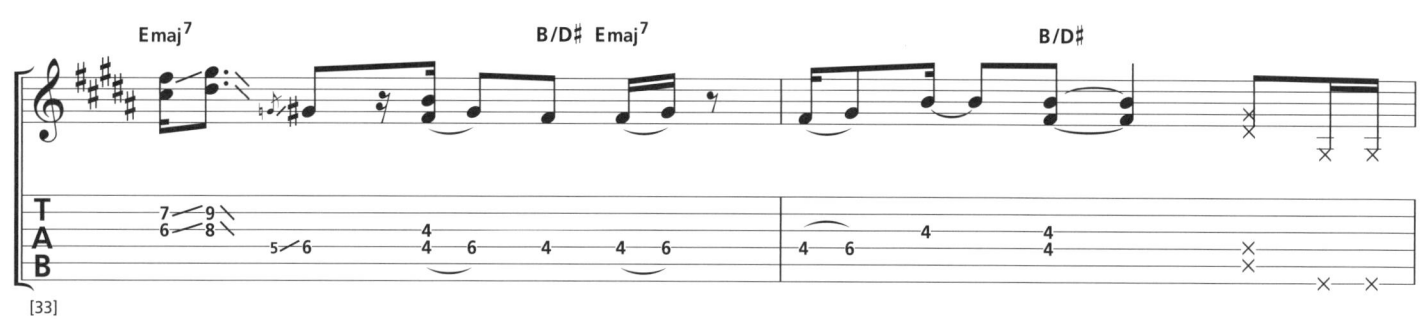
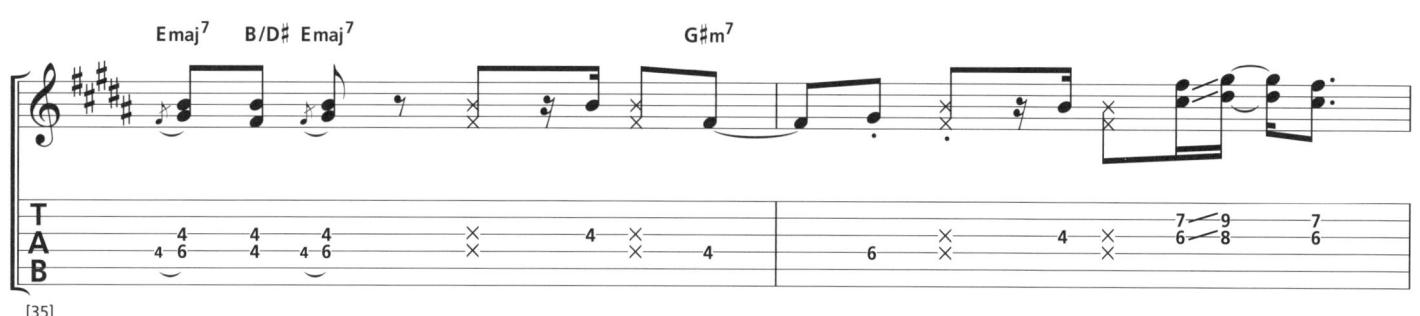
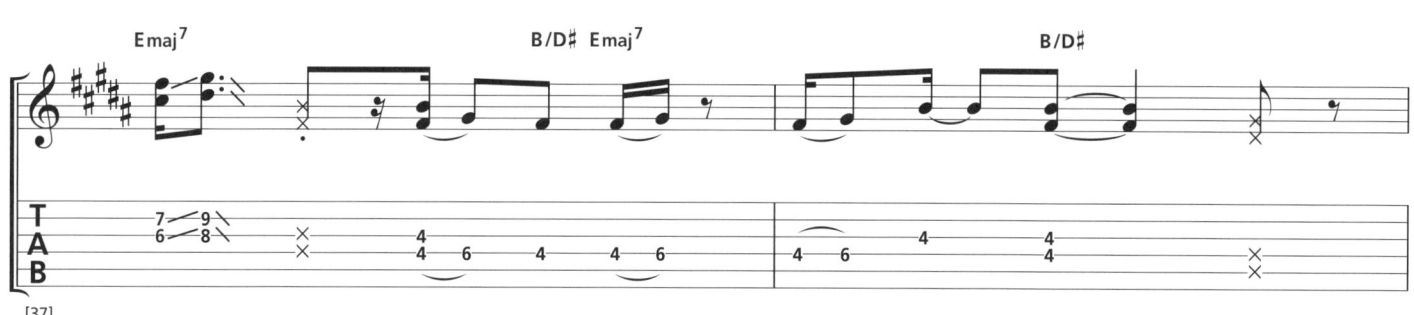
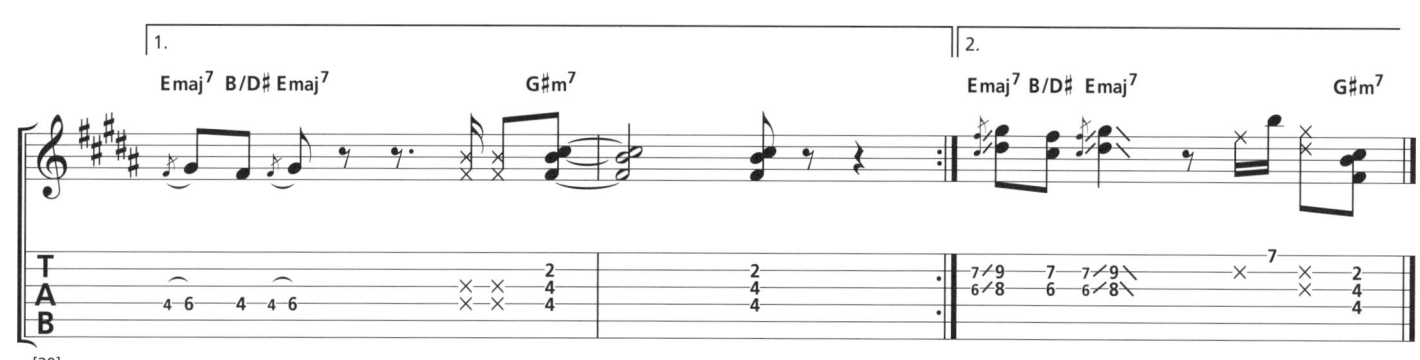

Walkthrough

Amp Settings

The tone should be very clean, and you could consider using a little compression to make the notes really 'pop'. Set the attack fairly fast and the sustain long. Single coil pickups or coiltapped humbuckers would be suitable, and it's best to stay away from neck pickups as they will be too warm and thick-sounding for this part.

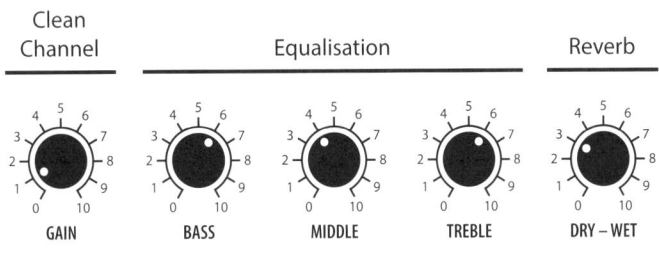

A Section (Measures 1–8)

This section sets up the groove for the whole song. This part wouldn't be out of place on a funk record from the 1970s. The part is mainly based on 4th double stops and, as we've discussed elsewhere, this is a staple of funk guitarists' vocabulary. Most of the notes in this part can be found within the B major pentatonic scale. The whole piece is within B major despite starting with an E major seventh chord. Prepare the rhythm carefully as the whole song is very syncopated. Remember the 16th note grid.

Measure 1

The first triple stop noteworthy in that it comprises a stack of two perfect 4ths, and from bottom to top these notes are the 6th, 9th and 5th over the E major 7 harmony. The second triple stop is made up of the same notes but shifted up a tone – here the notes are the major 7th, major 3rd, and the 6th. The next notes are perfect 4th double stops. Note that where the harmony has changed to B add 2 with the 3rd in the bass, the notes are often extensions of the underlying chords rather than chord tones. The approach here is really playing through the changes rather than thinking of each individual chord. Using the same material over moving chord changes shows real mastery of harmony.

B Section (Measures 9–24)

The rhythm of this part is clearly in keeping with the groove set up in the previous section. Again there is limited movement in the notes, the notes are all in the orbit of F♯ hammered onto G♯ with B held on top. It is very important to observe the note lengths here.

Measure 11

The note length is largely controlled by the left hand cutting off the note by slightly lifting off the fingerboard.

C Section (Measures 25–28)

The first two measures of this section just hold single notes. Note that he avoids the root with these single notes. Prince was very sophisticated with deep grounding in soul, R&B and rock.

Measure 27–28

This pattern is reminiscent of a bass guitar part, and played against a very sophisticated chord change – an F♯ triad over a G♯ bass. Prince was friendly with the great bass player Larry Graham and it's possible that his influence is evident here.

Cream

SONG TITLE: CROSSROADS
ALBUM: WHEELS OF FIRE
LABEL: POLYDOR/ATCO
GENRE: HARD ROCK / BLUES ROCK

WRITTEN BY: ROBERT JOHNSON
PRODUCED BY: FELIX PAPPALARDI

US CHART PEAK: 28

BACKGROUND INFO

'Crossroads' is the opening track of the live half of Cream's double album *Wheels Of Fire*, released in August 1968. The song was also released as a single after the band's breakup in January 1969. 'Crossroads' is an adaptation of the blues song written and recorded by Robert Johnson in 1936. The song is surrounded by mythology because it allegedly refers to the place where Johnson supposedly sold his soul to the devil in exchange for his musical gift. His lyrics do not make direct reference to this. Although there have been other recordings, such as Elmore James' 1954 and 1960–1961 versions, it is Eric Clapton's version, as recorded by Cream, that is the most covered. It is considered a seminal rock and roll piece.

Robert Johnson recorded 'Cross Road Blues' in San Antonio, Texas, in November 1936. He recorded two versions. Clapton's version was developed whilst he was a member of John Mayall's Bluesbreakers and he first recorded it with an ad hoc band that included Steve Winwood on vocals and Jack Bruce on bass. Clapton amalgamated lyrics from 'Crossroads' and 'Traveling Riverside Blues'. The song was played regularly by John Mayall's Bluesbreakers and Clapton brought it over to Cream in July 1966. He turned 'Crossroads' into a rock song using its core riff as the centrepiece for it. Cream added a heady improvisational approach bringing jazz elements reflected in Ginger Baker's complex drumming and Jack Bruce's syncopated bass playing. Despite Cream's extensively reworked version the song is credited to Robert Johnson. Cream had a short lived but highly influential career.

Eric Clapton is regarded as one of rock and roll's most important guitarists and is amongst a small group of instrumentalists who became the blueprint for aspiring lead guitarists. He was an advanced player by the age of 16 and his fluid and lyrical blues based delivery has been admired and imitated all over the world. In a career spanning over 50 years he has played with a who's who of the popular music world and toured all over the planet. Clapton has played the Royal Albert Hall over 200 times.

Eric Clapton is the recipient of 18 Grammy Awards and has sold nearly 130 million records worldwide.

Crossroads

Cream
Words & Music by Robert Johnson

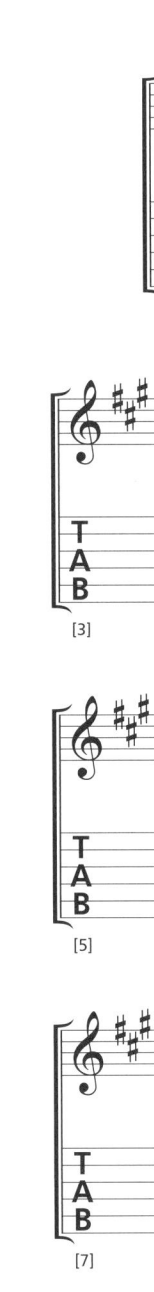

Arranged by Eric Clapton
© Copyright 1969 Eric Clapton.
Print Rights Administered by Hal Leonard LLC.
All Rights Reserved. International Copyright Secured.

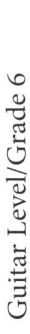

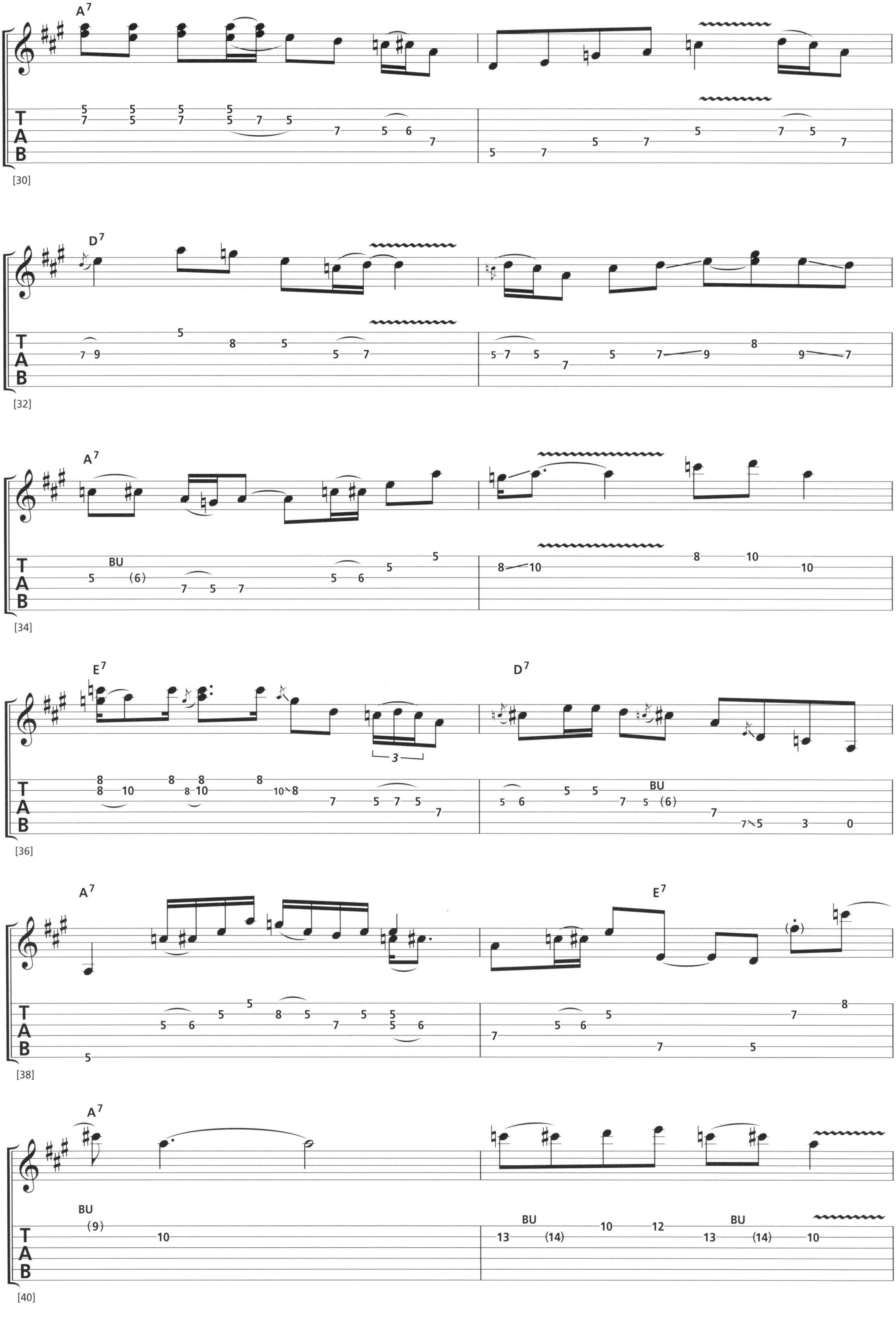
A7
[30]
D7
[32]
A7
BU
[34]
E7
D7
BU
[36]
A7
E7
[38]
A7
BU
BU
BU
[40]

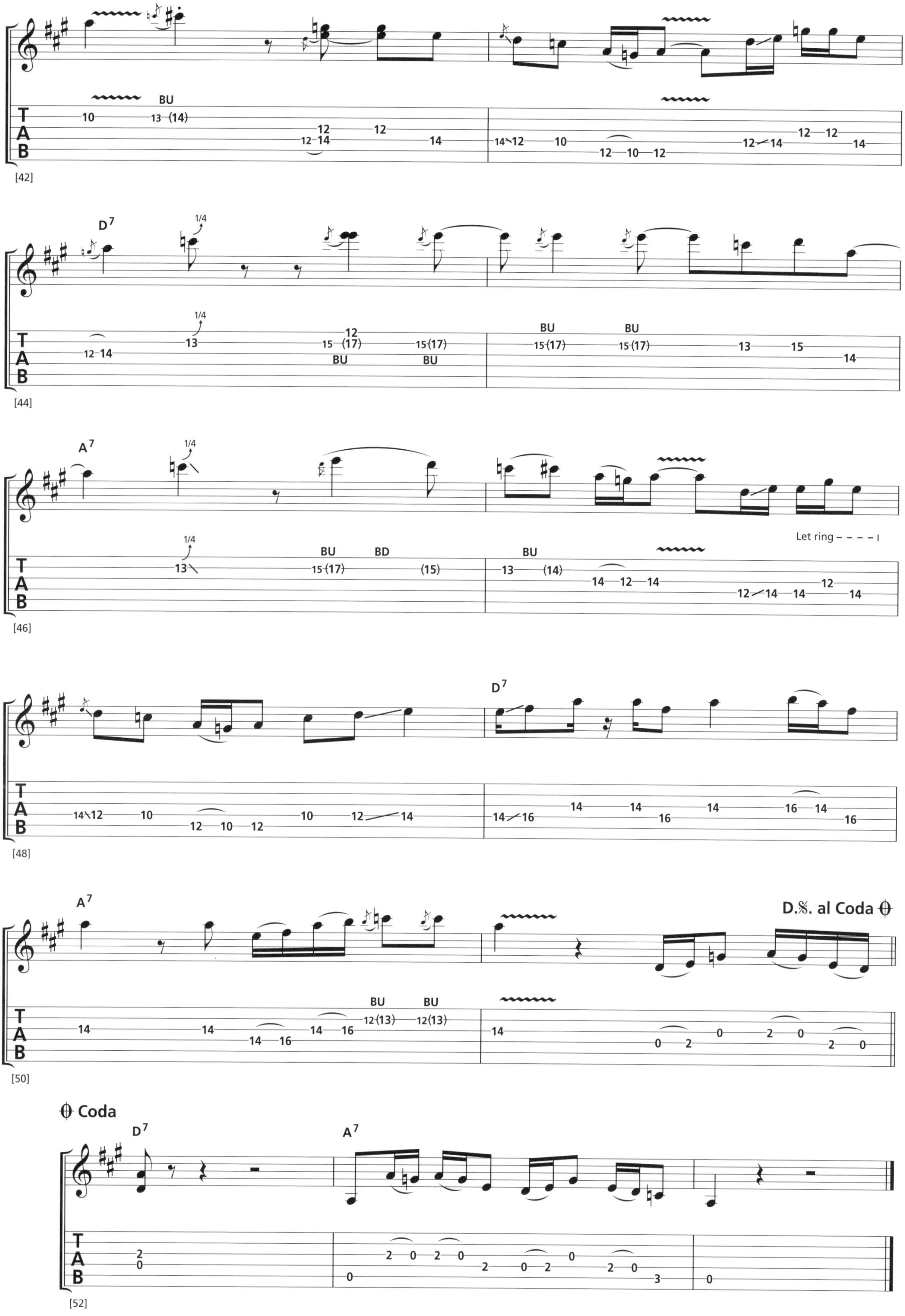
[42]
BU
D7
1/4
BU
[44]
A7
1/4
BU
BD
Let ring
[46]
D7
[48]
A7
D.𝄋. al Coda 𝄌
BU
[50]
𝄌 Coda
D7
A7
[52]

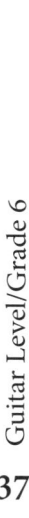

Walkthrough

Amp Settings

The amp should be a classic late 1970s British model if possible otherwise try and simulate this sound as best you can with your existing amp. Overdrive is essential whether it comes from your amp or from a pedal. Eric was using a classic solid bodied two pickup humbucker guitar.

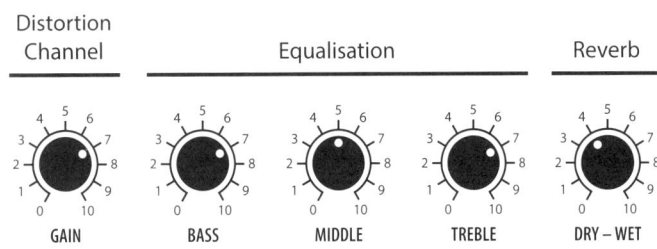

Intro Section (Measures 1–12)

This is an iconic groove, and classic high energy blues-rock. Eric's arrangement is quite different in approach from Robert Johnson's original version, and demonstrates his astonishing abilities as a blues improviser.

Measure 11

Eric subtly states the major third here, making great use of minor-major 3rd hammer-ons. Many blues players learned to follow the change from the I to the IV chord by using the major pentatonic over the I, moving to a minor pentatonic on the same root to cover the IV. For instance, the C♯ of the major pentatonic is found in the A^7 chord whereas D^7 has the note C♮.

Verse section (Measures 13–27)

Here Eric is playing rhythm under his own vocal. Concentrate on really locking in with the underlying pulse. The best way to do this is to be aware of the subdivisions of the beat.

Solo Section (Measures 28–51)

The pickup to this solo in measure 27 introduces a strong extension of the chord tones – F♯ which is the sixth degree of A and is in the A major pentatonic. Robben Ford makes great use of this note in his solos.

Measures 28–29

This solo segment is strongly based on the A major pentatonic, bringing Freddie King's guitar style to mind. The great blues guitar players often play definite phrases and take care to express them in a musical way. Clapton, like B.B. King before him, is a master of conversational development within a solo. It often sounds like he starts with a question and follows with an answering phrase.

Measure 30

The parts in this measure have something of a Jimi Hendrix quality to them. Eric is seeking extra notes around the shape of the underlying chord – in this case A^7, and this is a basic form of what jazz players would call 'chord melody'. As his guitar was functioning as the only chordal instrument in the trio (although bass can in someways be considered a harmony instrument), Eric was interspersing his solos with chordal ideas (even double stops) in order to embellish the musical texture.

Measures 31–33

Here Eric breaks out of the A minor pentatonic and suddenly the solo takes on a more bluesy colour. He follows this scale in the next two measures over the D^7 chord.

Measure 34

This is a perfect example of the effect of the major pentatonic on the I chord. Practise the bend carefully, and check the C♯ by sounding it as a fretted note before attempting to bend into it from C♮.

Measures 34–35

Here Eric starts with the major pentatonic and moves to the minor pentatonic for a bluesy edge. Check out the vibrato on the A notes – Eric's technique is exemplary. Vibrato is a huge component of a guitar player's tone.

Mohair Mountain

SONG TITLE: MOHAIR MOUNTAIN
GENRE: CLASSIC ROCK
TEMPO: 92/126 BPM
KEY: A MINOR

TECH FEATURES: TIME SIGNATURE CHANGES
TEMPO CHANGE
SOLOING WITH DYNAMICS

COMPOSERS: JOE BENNETT
& KUNG FU DRUMMER

PERSONNEL: STUART RYAN (GTR)
HENRY THOMAS (BASS)
NOAM LEDERMAN (DRUMS)

OVERVIEW

'Mohair Mountain' is a classic rock piece similar in style to the pioneering sounds of classic rock bands such as Cream, Led Zeppelin and Aerosmith. Among its techniques it features time signature changes, legato runs and soloing with dynamics.

STYLE FOCUS

Classic rock guitar is influenced by electric blues. For example, the most common scales in classic rock lead playing and riff writing are the minor pentatonic and its close relative the blues scale. String bends, vibrato and other nuances come directly from the blues. Faster passages are not usually played using strict alternate picking. Instead they feature hammer-ons and pull-offs that are, generally speaking, less demanding in terms of technique.

THE BIGGER PICTURE

There's a distinct thread connecting the electric blues of the 1950s and 1960s to classic rock. Blues guitarists developed a style of playing that utilised the relatively low tension and height of electric guitar strings compared to the set-up of the traditional acoustic or semi-acoustic instruments. Electric guitars are made for string bends, which make for a vocal-like sound custom-built for the expressiveness of the blues. English groups like The Rolling Stones, The Yardbirds and Cream all reinterpreted the parts they heard on blues records, thus creating blues rock.

Eric Clapton was the pivotal figure in the blues rock scene. On John Mayall's 1966 album *Blues Breakers With Eric Clapton* he demonstrated a great understanding of electric blues and a virtuoso technique. His impressive tone was achieved by turning up his Marshall amp until it distorted under the yoke of a humbucker equipped Gibson Les Paul. Led Zeppelin's Jimmy Page used the same set-up to fuel many riffs like 'Black Dog' and 'Heartbreaker'.

Today, Black Country Communion, Black Stone Cherry and Kasabian continue to fill stadiums with guitar riffs inspired by classic rock.

RECOMMENDED LISTENING

Led Zeppelin's 'Black Dog' and 'The Ocean' both use time signature tricks with riffs. The Doors' 'Roadhouse Blues' is a strong and simple example of a blues boogie riff in a rock song, and Kasabian's 'Shoot The Runner' is a more recent version of a similar idea.

Mohair Mountain

Joe Bennett & Kung Fu Drummer

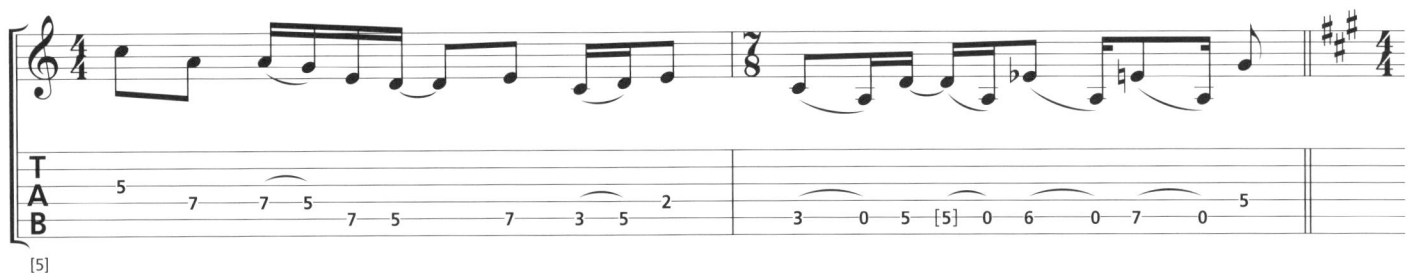
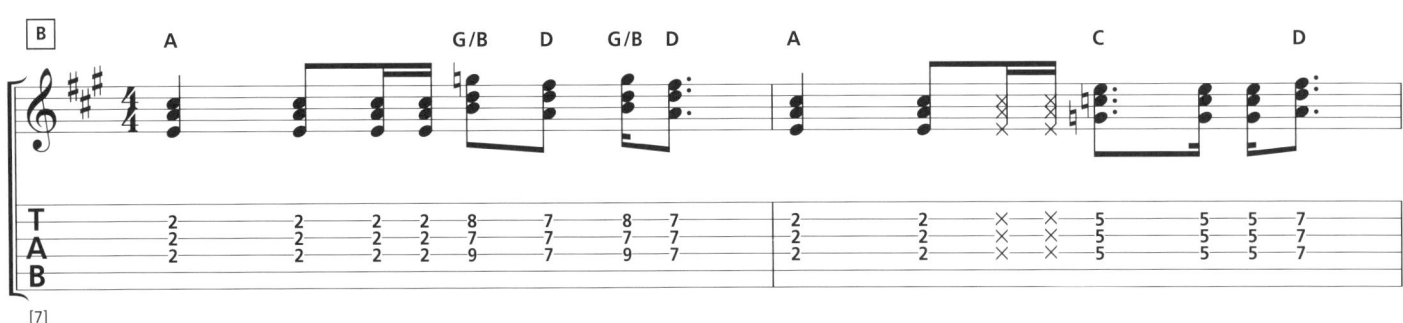
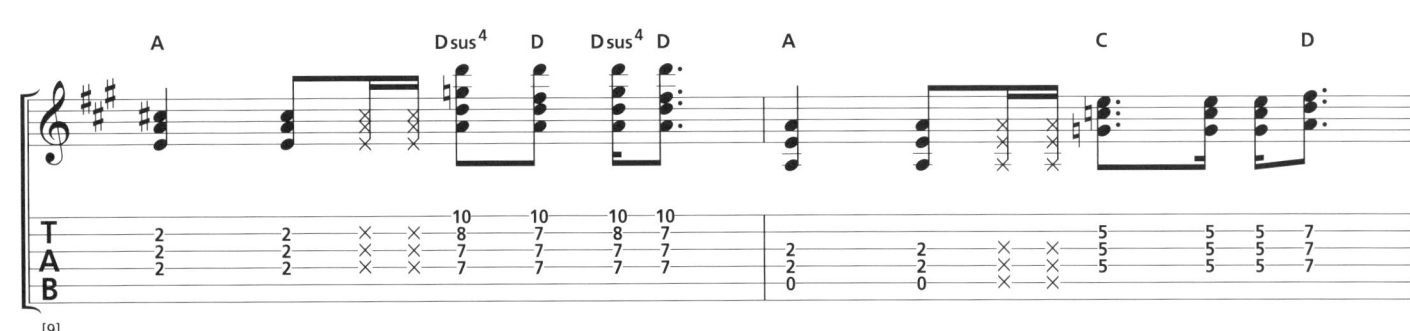

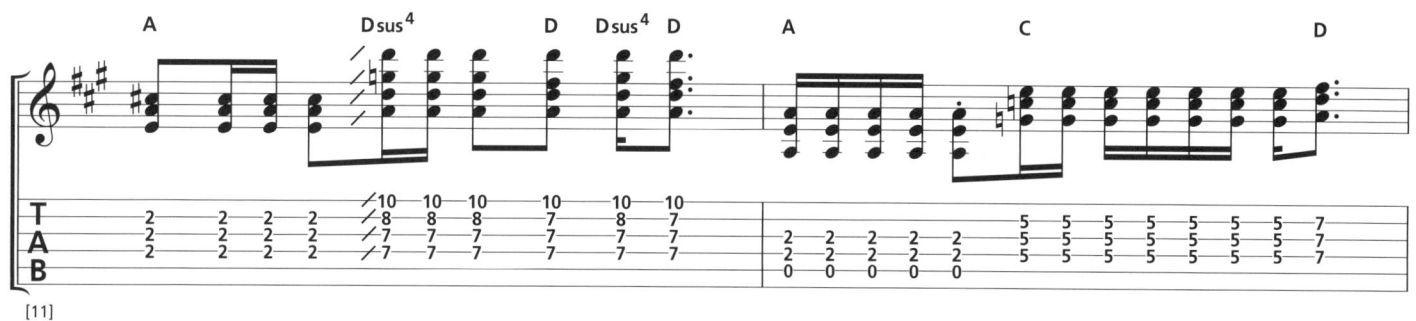
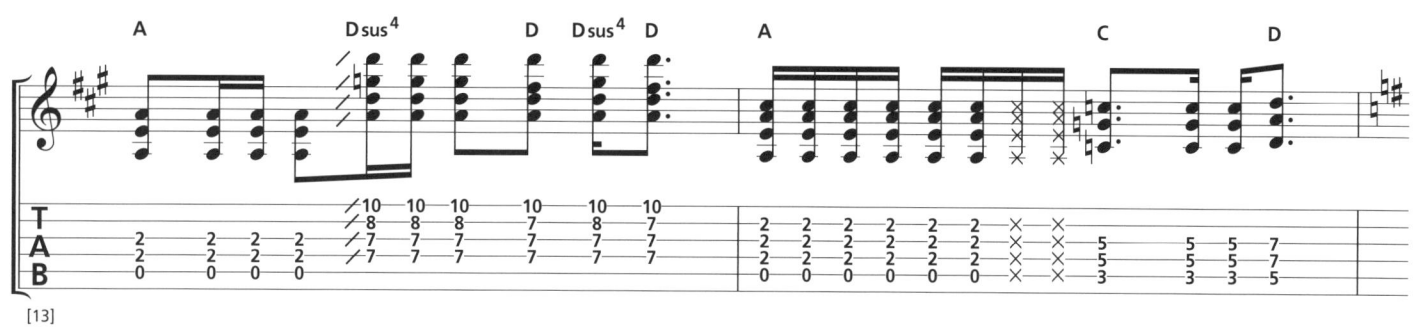

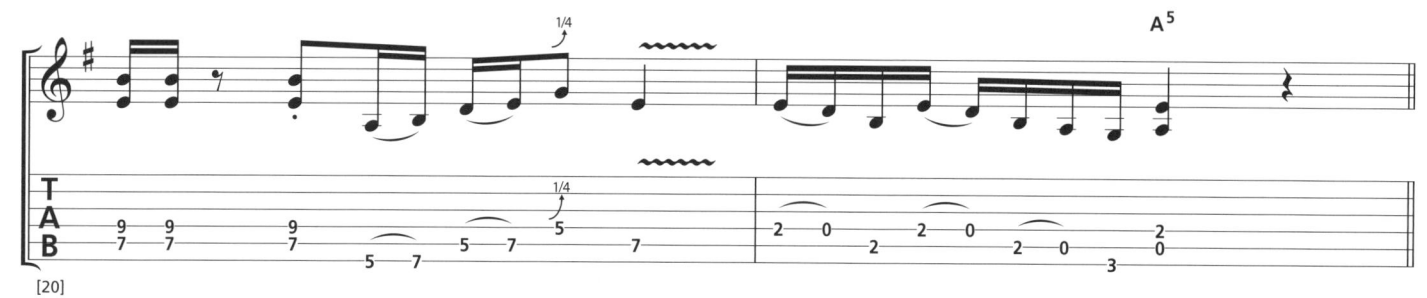

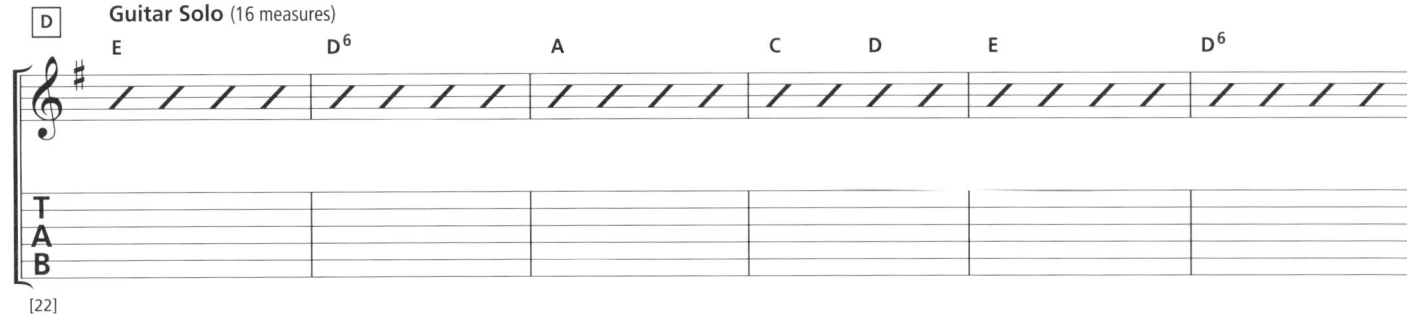
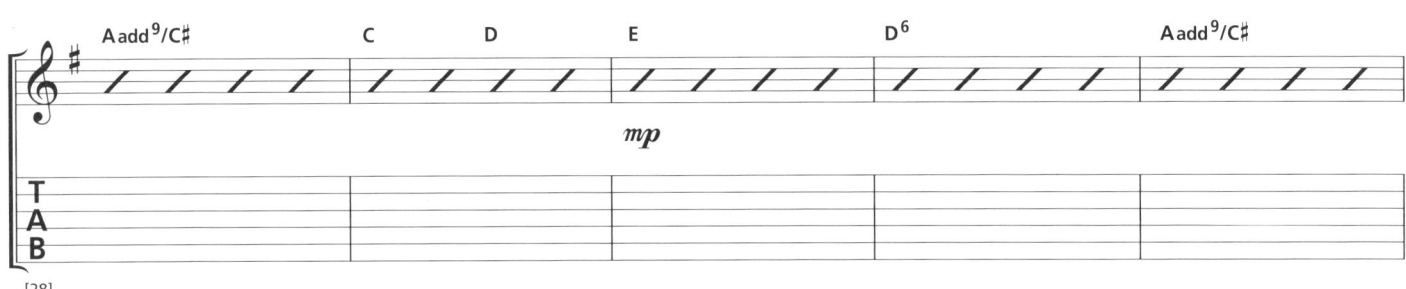
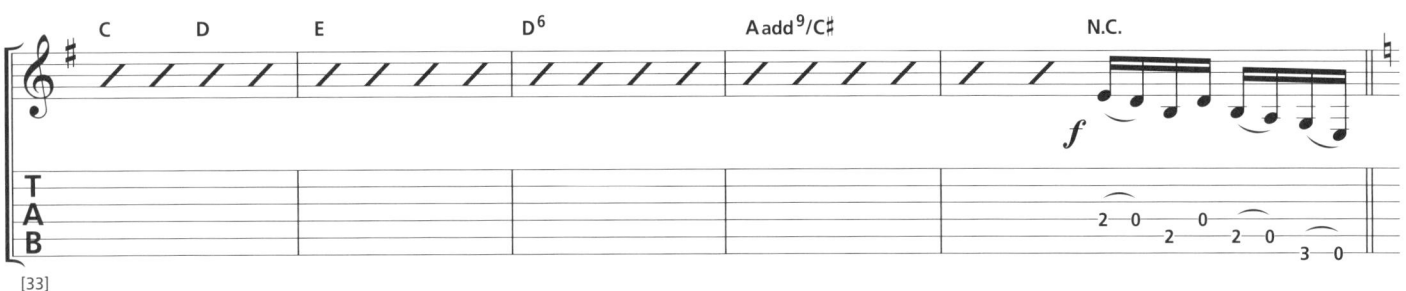

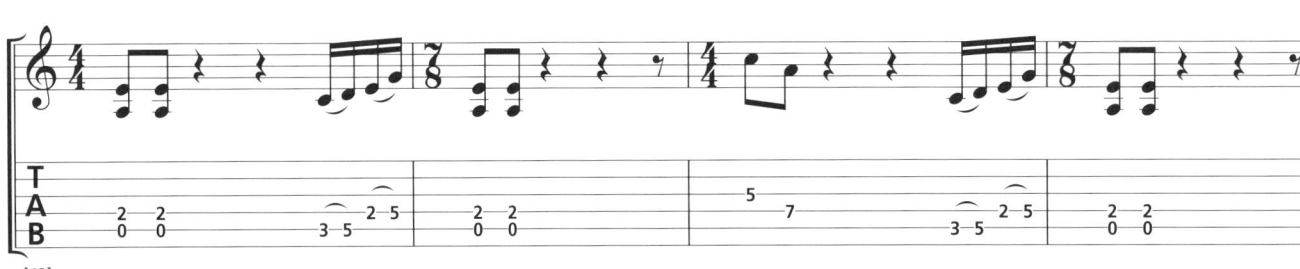

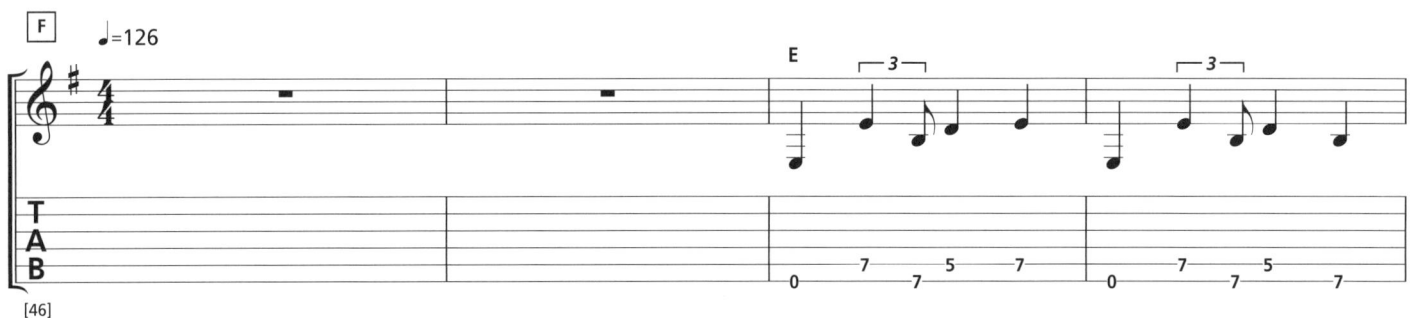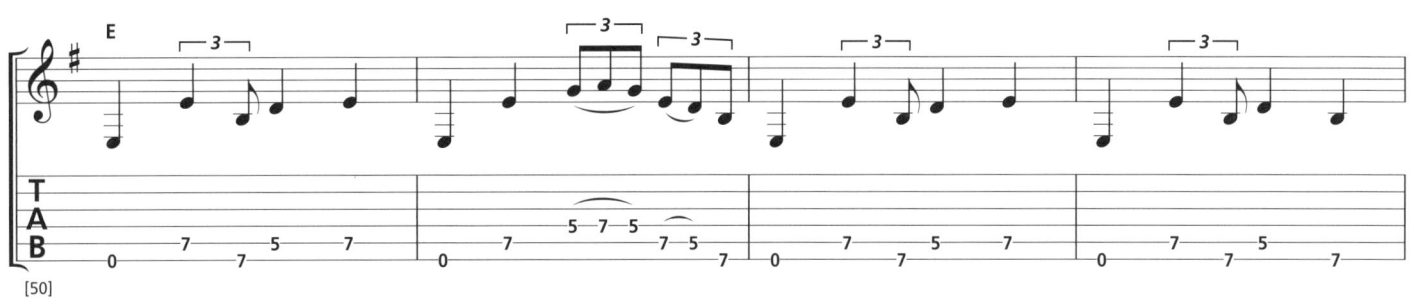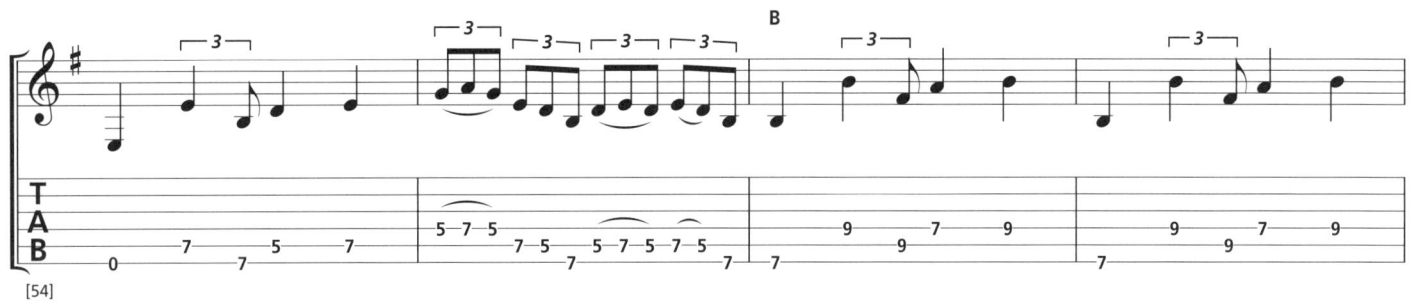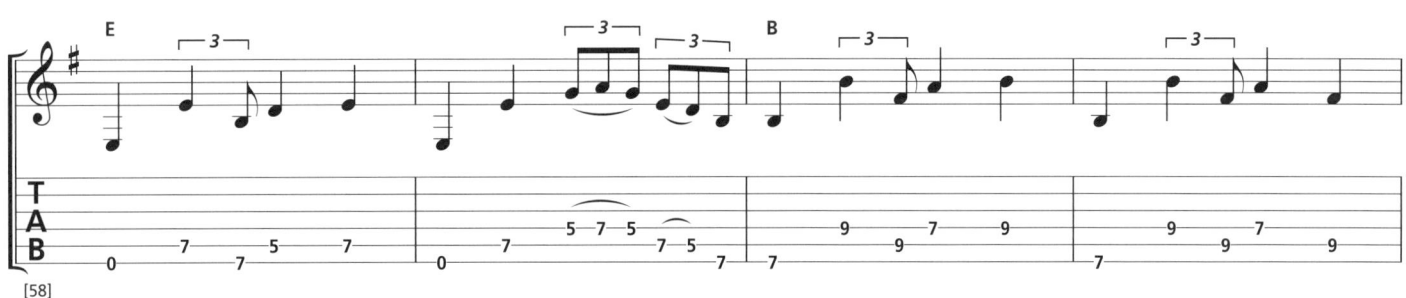

Walkthrough

Amp Settings
The overdriven guitar sound is not as heavily saturated as it first appears, so avoid the temptation to add too much distortion/gain. Boost the middle and treble to give your tone an aggressive edge that will cut through the mix.

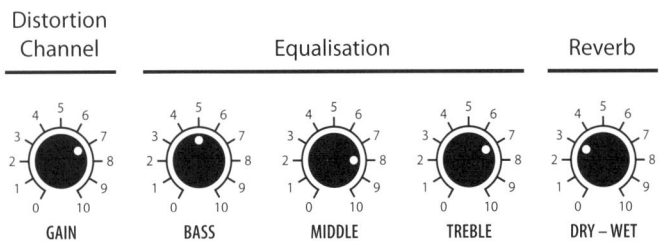

A Section (Measures 1–6)
The A Section is a single-note riff using extensive hammer-ons and pull-offs. The most challenging aspect of this riff is the movement between 4/4 and 7/8 time signatures.

Measures 1–6 | *4/4 to 7/8 time signature change*
It's common to count 4/4 as "1 & 2 & 3 & 4 &" and 7/8 as "one-two-three-four-five-six-sev". However, since the pulse of the track doesn't shift to eighth notes from this measure, another way to think of the 7/8 is to treat it as a measure of 4/4 with half a beat missing. Omit the '&' count from beat 4 to help you feel the groove more (Fig. 1).

B Section (Measures 7–14)
This chordal riff moves a single chord shape around the fretboard using embellishments to create extra movement.

Measures 7–14 | *Ghost strums*
A constant 16th-note strumming motion help create fluency. When you don't want to strike the strings, move your pick away a small amount so your hand passes over the strings without striking them – these are ghost strums.

C Section (Measures 15–21)
Here you combine single-note pentatonic ideas with two-note chords.

Measures 15–18 | *Three on four rhythm*
These measures feature a rhythmic idea where a three-beat pattern is placed across the 4/4 time signature to create interesting accents (Fig. 2). It may help to count through the measures so that you don't lose where the strong beats are.

D Section (Measures 22–37)
The D section is a guitar solo and features a change of dynamics halfway through.

Measures 22–37 | *Guitar solo*
Stylistically, the blues or minor pentatonic scales are the most obvious choices. However, this solo is about more than scale choices. Eight measures in the dynamic changes from f to mp and it is important that your solo reflects this.

E Section (Measures 38–45)
This is a John Bonham (Led Zeppelin) style drum solo where the guitar plays a sparser variation of the A section.

Measures 38–45 | *Tight rhythm parts*
The combination of changing time signatures and the large number of rests means it is essential that you count through the measures here. If you tap your foot, be aware that the 7/8 measure will interrupt the flow of these movements.

F Section (Measures 46–64)
This single-note riff has a triplet feel and a change of tempo.

Measures 46–64 | *Tempo change*
The first two measures of the tempo change are first played by the bass and then the drums. Use these two measures to get settled into the new tempo/groove.

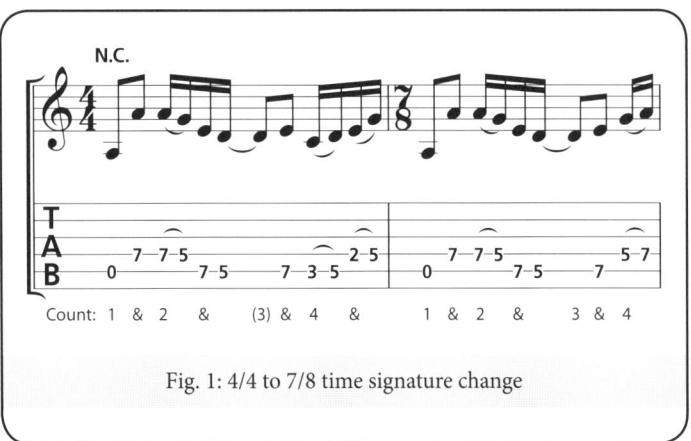

Fig. 1: 4/4 to 7/8 time signature change

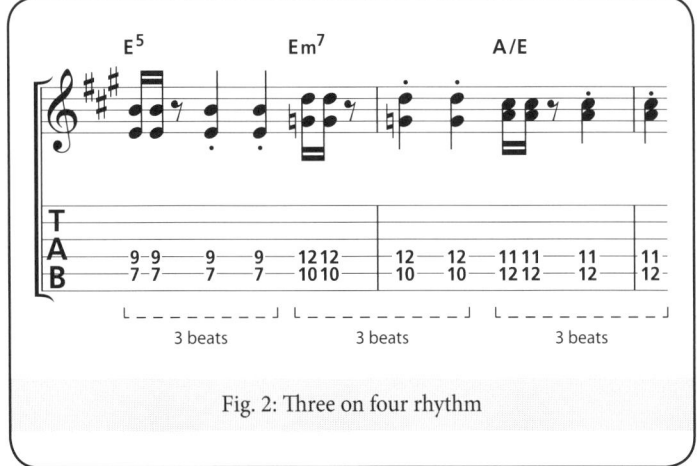

Fig. 2: Three on four rhythm

Striped Shirt

SONG TITLE: STRIPED SHIRT
GENRE: JAZZ
TEMPO: 96 BPM
KEY: B MINOR

TECH FEATURES: SLASH CHORDS
CHORD MELODY PLAYING
OCTAVE MELODY PLAYING

COMPOSER: KIT MORGAN

PERSONNEL: LARRY CARLTON (GTR)
HENRY THOMAS (BASS)
NOAM LEDERMAN (DRUMS)
ROSS STANLEY (KEYS)
FERGUS GERRAND (PERC)

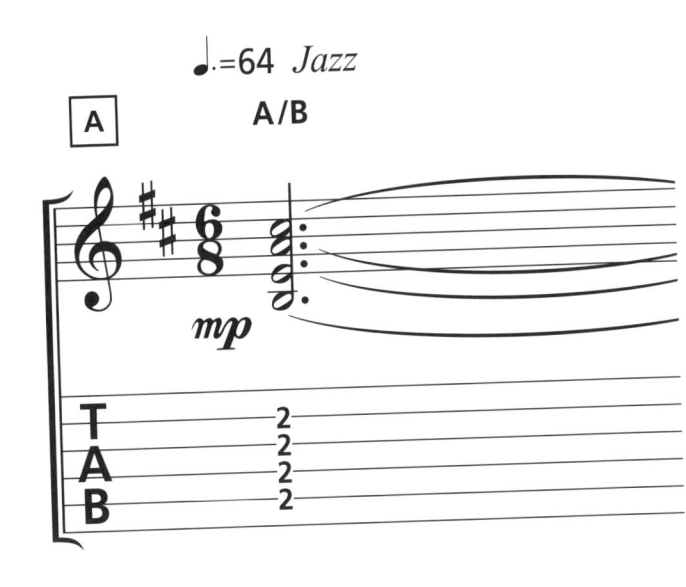

OVERVIEW

'Striped Shirt' is a jazz composition inspired by the American guitarist Pat Metheny, and played by the great session player and solo fusion artist Larry Carlton. As with Metheny's writing, this piece is full of harmonic sophistication. Although rooted in the key of B minor, there are slash chord voicings where the bass note is not the root of the chord, as well as some non-diatonic chords (i.e. chords that do not belong to the key).

STYLE FOCUS

Metheny has developed his own sound within the jazz genre, fusing traditional elements of bebop with world music including Brazilian bossa nova. Labelling him a 'smooth jazz' player does him little credit. His vast output has explored many different styles from bebop to atonal jazz and film score work. Sophisticated chord voicings and less than obvious harmony are also hallmarks of his tasteful style.

THE BIGGER PICTURE

Metheny is regarded by many as one of the world's greatest jazz guitarists. He fuses incredible technique with a sophisticated harmonic knowledge and superb compositional abilities. He was born in Kansas in 1954, and was playing and teaching guitar professionally by the time he was 18.

His early work in a trio with virtuoso bassist Jaco Pastorius brought him to the attention of the world's jazz audience, and he has achieved phenomenal success as leader of the Pat Metheny Group touring the world and performing in arenas and stadiums, a feat unheard of for a jazz artist. Metheny can be heard playing anything from archtop jazz guitar, synth, acoustic steel string and nylon string, to his unique Linda Manzer designed 42-string Pikasso guitar.

RECOMMENDED LISTENING

Metheny's early trio recordings, especially his debut *Bright Size Life* (1976), hinted at the development of a major voice in jazz guitar. He found his feet as leader of the Pat Metheny Group and his writing with keys player Lyle Mays is expressive and lyrical. The trio's live album *The Road To You* (1993) boasts his stellar guitar work. He is also a wonderfully intimate performer and his acoustic duets album with Charlie Haden, *Beyond The Missouri Sky (Short Stories)* (1997), is a personal recording of two masters and friends performing with lyricism and restraint.

Striped Shirt

Kit Morgan

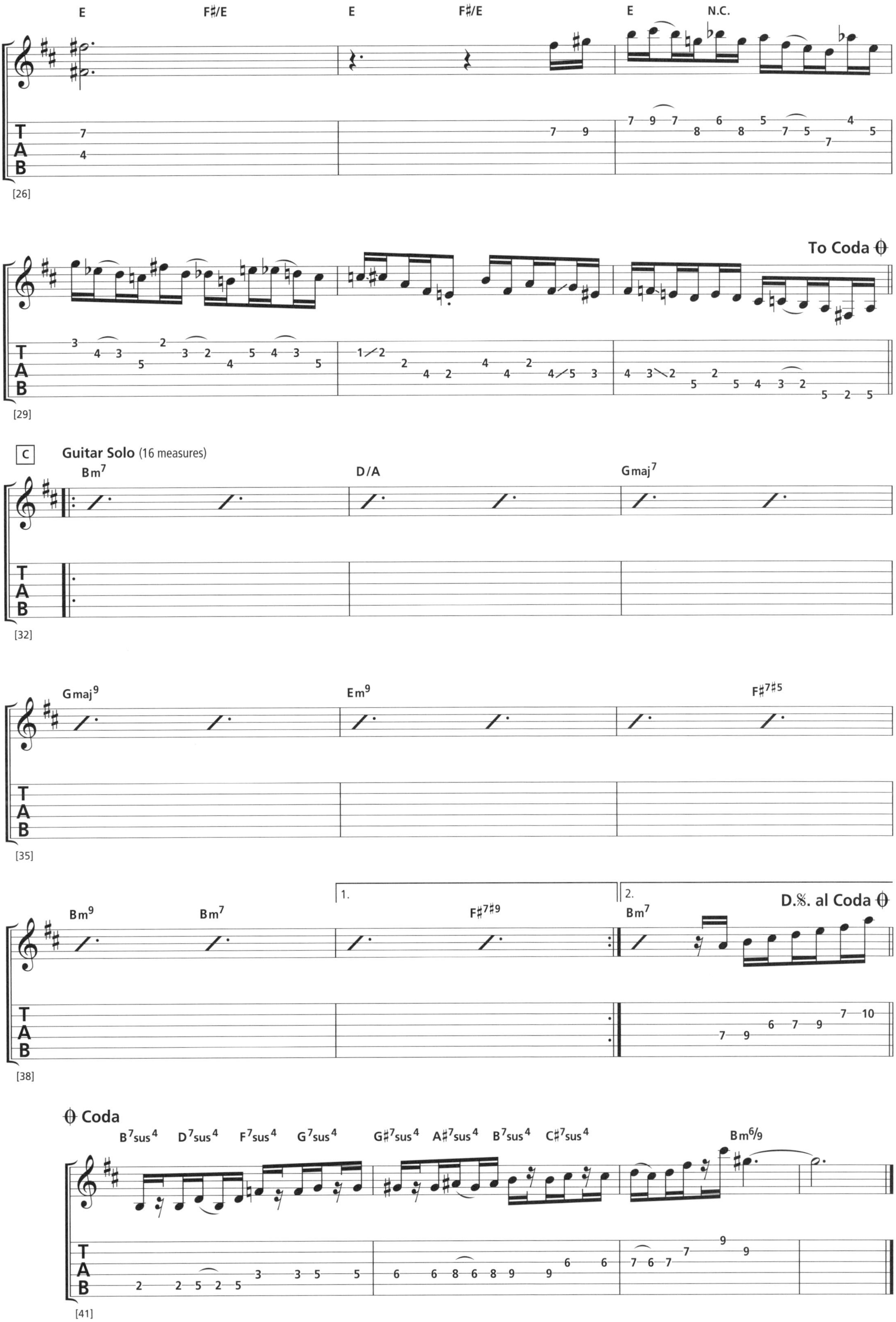
E F♯/E E F♯/E E N.C.
[26]
To Coda
[29]
C Guitar Solo (16 measures)
Bm7 D/A Gmaj7
[32]
Gmaj9 Em9 F♯7♯5
[35]
1. 2.
D.%. al Coda
Bm9 Bm7 F♯7♯9 Bm7
[38]
Coda
B7sus4 D7sus4 F7sus4 G7sus4 G♯7sus4 A♯7sus4 B7sus4 C♯7sus4 Bm6/9
[41]

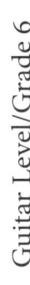

Walkthrough

Amp Settings
Go for a full, well-rounded tone for this song. You may find that the neck pickup will be the best choice for 'Striped Shirt' because it has the thickest tone. A generous amount reverb will enhance the melodic parts.

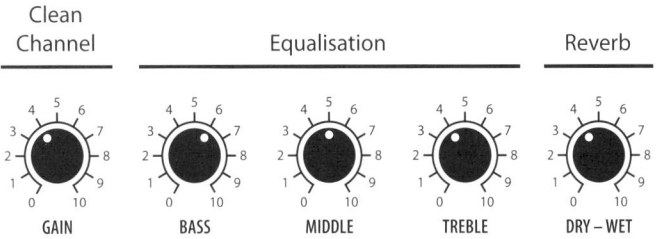

A Section (Measures 1–13)
The A section starts with sustained chords then moves to a melody that is created by picking notes from chord shapes.

Measures 1–44 | *6/8 time signature*
6/8 differs from 4/4 in that, instead of having a pulse of four beats per measure that is usually divided into multiples of two, it has a pulse of two beats divided into multiples of three.

Measures 1–44 | *Complex rhythms*
There are many rhythms in this piece that are complex, but some are easier to master by ear than the notation suggests. Listen to the audio and you should find that most of the phrases come naturally. If you find a phrase challenging, work out where against the count the notes fall and play through the phrase slowly, counting as you go (Fig. 1).

Measures 5–9 | *Picking options*
There are two picking options here. Some players may wish to play them fingerstyle. However, you will need to switch quickly back to plectrum playing at the end of the phrase. Alternatively, use hybrid picking to play the phrases.

Measure 5 | *Hybrid picking*
Hold the pick as normal between your thumb and index finger, keeping your hand relaxed. Pick the A string and pluck the B string with your ring finger. It should strike the string at a slightly diagonal angle, moving up towards the heel of your thumb. You can play the remainder of the phrase using the pick or with hybrid picking (Fig. 2).

B Section (Measures 14–31)
The B section is a flowing octave melody where each phrase is preceded by an ascending single-note phrase. The section ends with a challenging descending run.

Measures 27–31 | *Descending run*
It's best to deal with this phrase a beat at a time. Start slowly, gradually connecting the individual beats together before the connecting measures. Using a clean tone will make any slips in accuracy immediately audible, so don't increase the speed until you can play the beat or measure without errors.

C Section (Measures 32–40)
The C section is the guitar solo, where you will find some interesting chords to play over.

Measures 32–40 | *Guitar solo*
The guitar solo, like the piece itself, is in the key of B minor and although there are some unusual chords (such as G maj^9 and F#$^{7\#5}$), the entire solo can be improvised over using just two scales. As well as the obvious minor pentatonic and blues scale choices, the natural minor scale will work over everything except the F# chords. Despite their complex names, the only note from both chords not found in the natural minor scale is the A#, so use the harmonic minor over these chords.

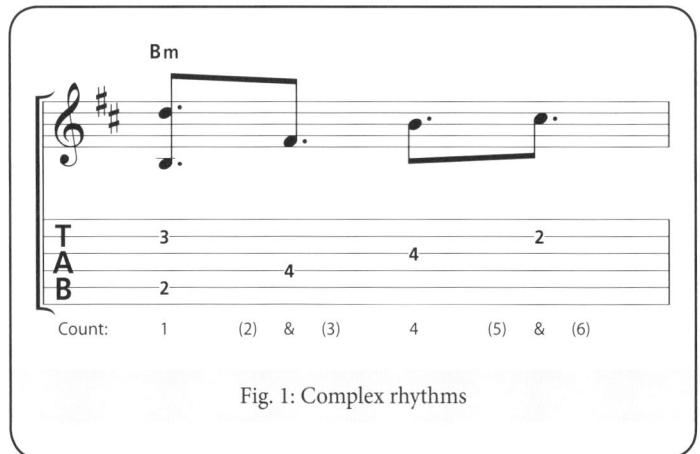

Fig. 1: Complex rhythms

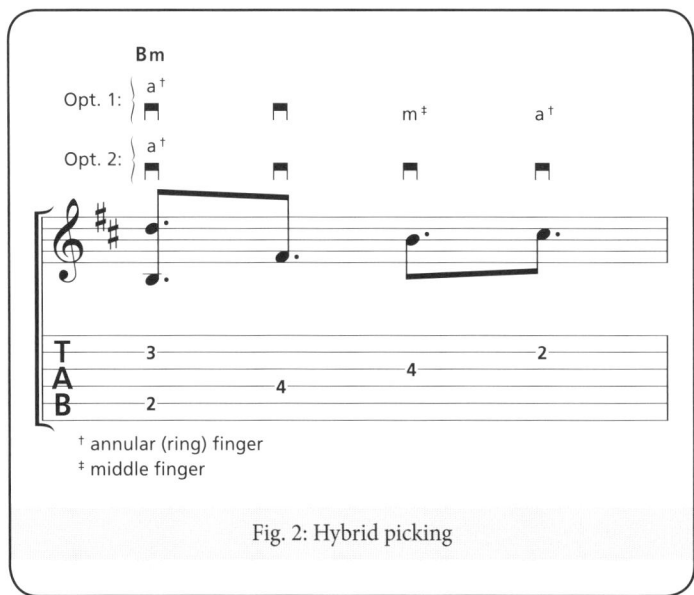

† annular (ring) finger
‡ middle finger

Fig. 2: Hybrid picking

That Sounds Like Noise

SONG TITLE: THAT SOUNDS LIKE NOISE
GENRE: FUNK ROCK
TEMPO: 86 BPM
KEY: F# DORIAN (MODAL)

TECH FEATURES: PINCHED HARMONICS
SWUNG 16TH NOTES
TWO-HAND TAPPING

COMPOSER: JAMES UINGS

PERSONNEL: JAMES UINGS (GTR)
DAVE MARKS (BASS)
NOAM LEDERMAN (DRUMS)

OVERVIEW

'That Sounds Like Noise' is a funk rock piece in the style of Steve Vai, Rage Against The Machine (RATM) and Extreme. It features pinched harmonics, swung 16th notes, two-hand tapping and slides.

STYLE FOCUS

Unlike traditional funk, funk rock doesn't usually include scratchy 16th-note strumming patterns. Distorted single-note riffs are more typical and, as is the case here, these are often comprised of 16th notes played with a swing feel. Certain techniques are borrowed from shred, including two-hand tapping, sweep-picking and extreme use of the whammy measure.

THE BIGGER PICTURE

During the late 1980s to early 1990s, several rock musicians combined rock riffs with funk rhythms. The resulting style was a new form of funk rock notable for a high-gain distortion that, at the time, was associated more with metal than funk.

Red Hot Chili Peppers, Fishbone and Living Colour were among the first wave of this new strain of funk rock. Although he was later to adopt a rock tone and technique, RHCP's John Frusciante flaunted a high-gain sound on the 1989 album *Mother's Milk* and gave thanks to shred guitarist Steve Vai in the liner notes.

Vai began his career in Frank Zappa's band. This virtuoso's contribution to the funk rock genre was the impressive instrumental track 'The Animal' from his 1990 album *Passion And Warfare*.

Like Vai, RATM's Tom Morello was dedicated to the art of shred. In the band he was known for his mimicry of hip hop turntable techniques, but his shred ability can be heard on the fluid legato of his solo on 'Know Your Enemy'.

Extreme were operating around the same time as RATM and in Nuno Bettencourt they had a guitarist who could shred and funk with equal aplomb.

RECOMMENDED LISTENING

RHCP's *Mother's Milk* shows Frusciante at his most technical and metal sounding. 'Lil Jack Horny' from Extreme's *Extreme II: Pornograffitti* (1990) demonstrates a swung 16th note feel, and RATM's eponymous debut (1993) is littered with Morello's inventive guitar playing.

That Sounds Like Noise

James Uings

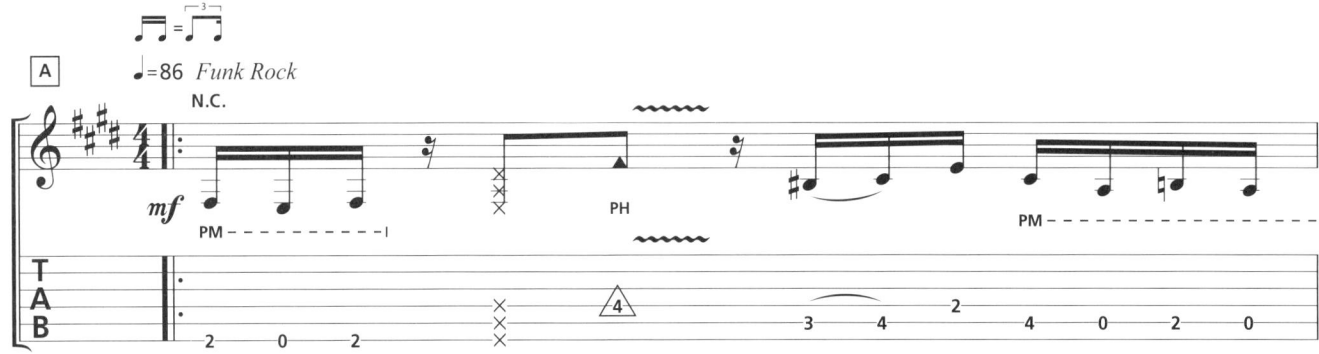
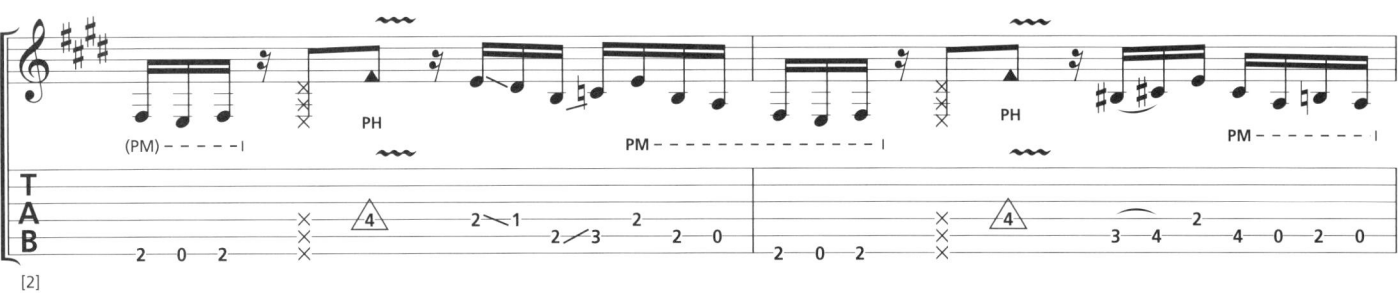

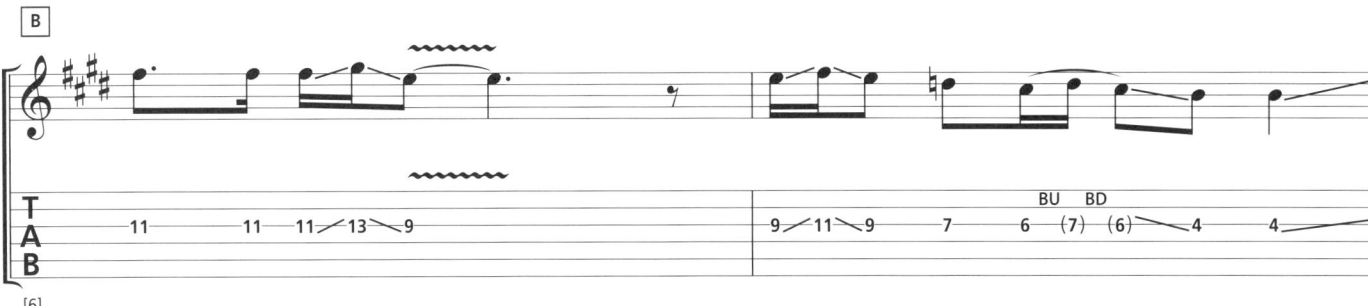

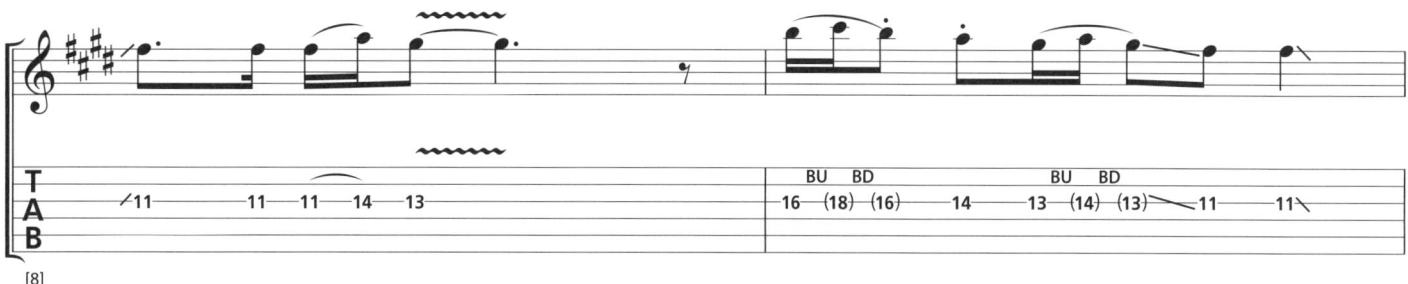

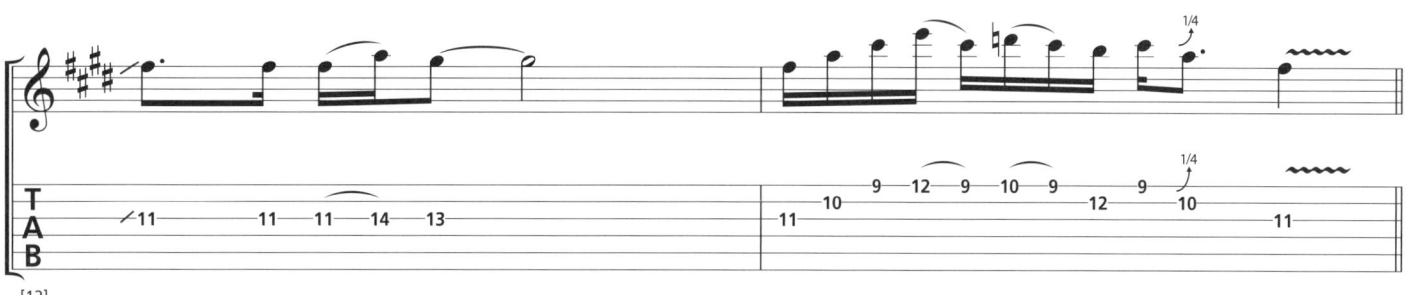
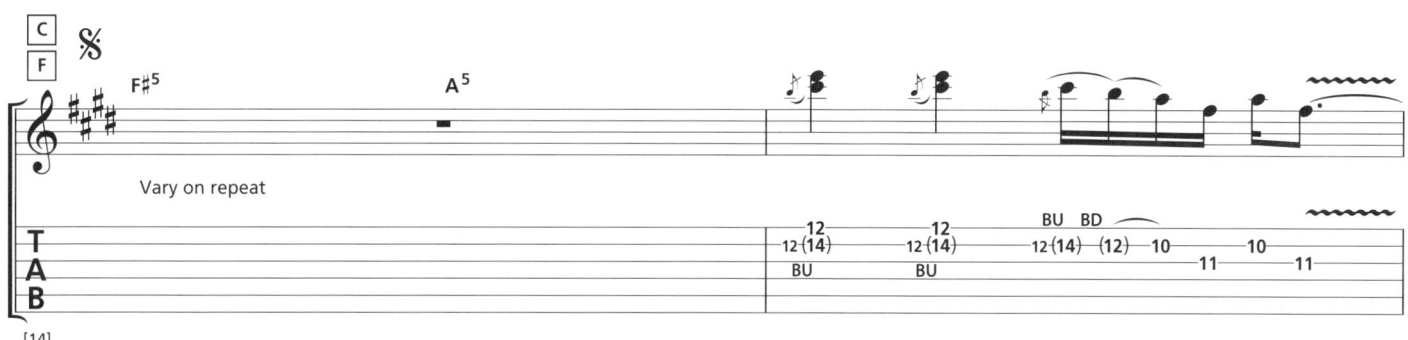
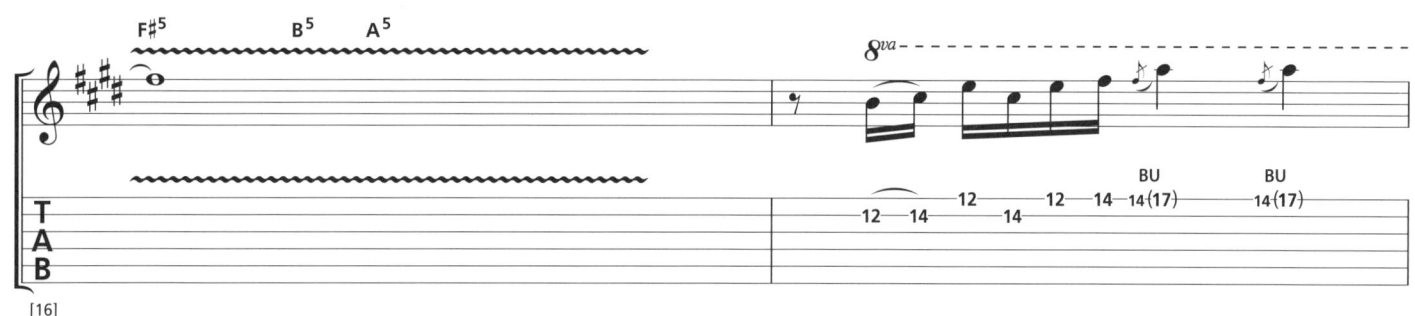

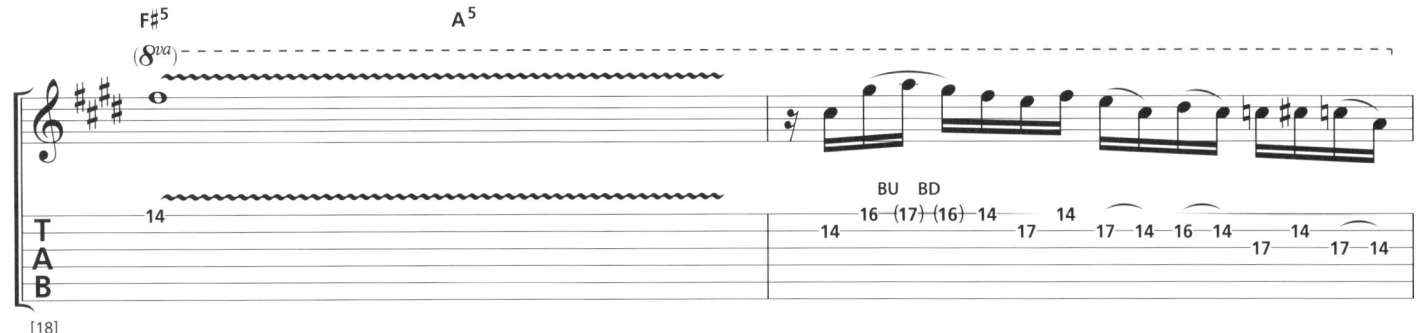
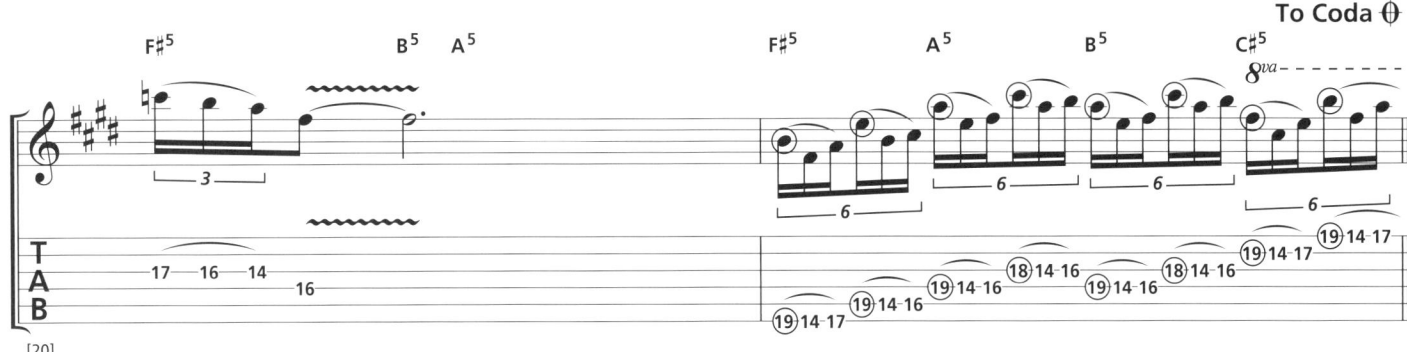
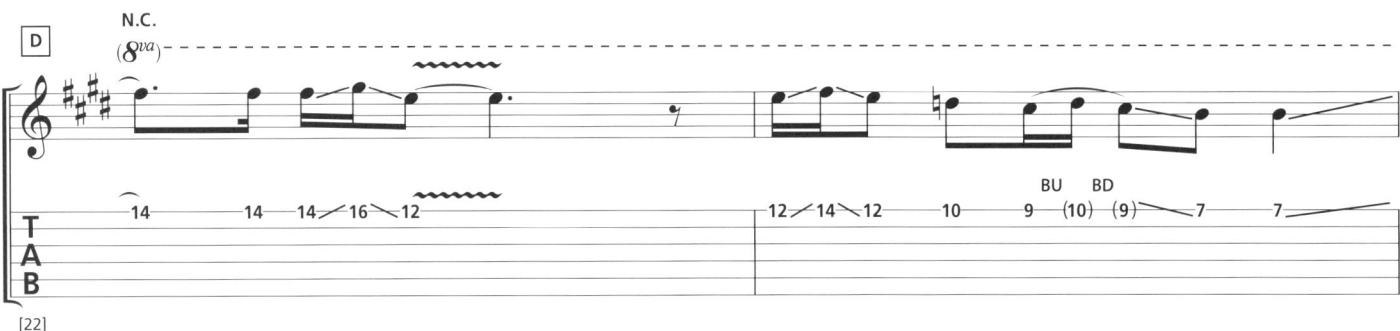

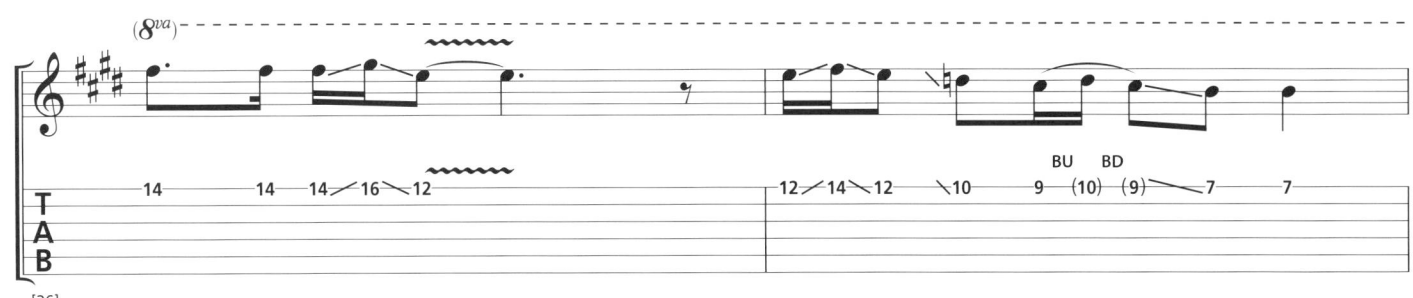

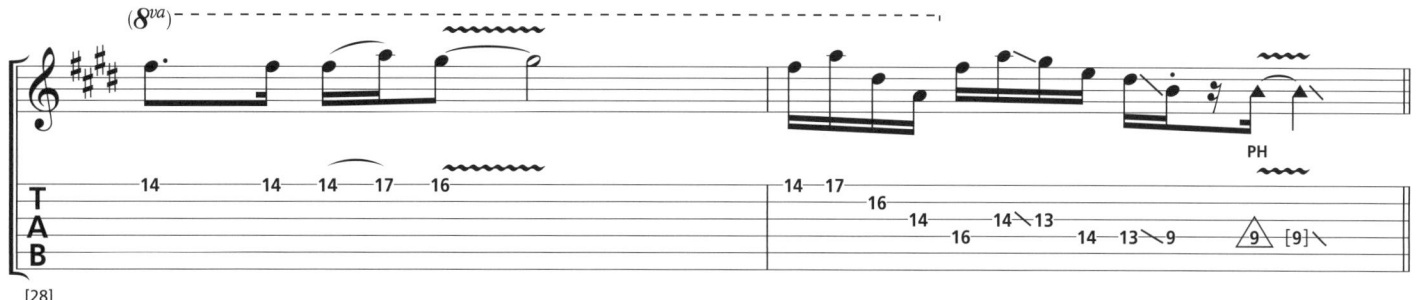

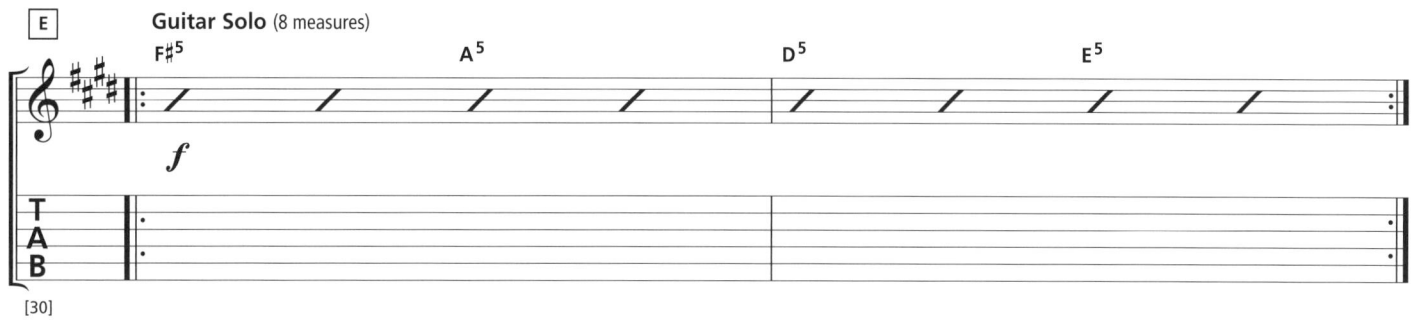

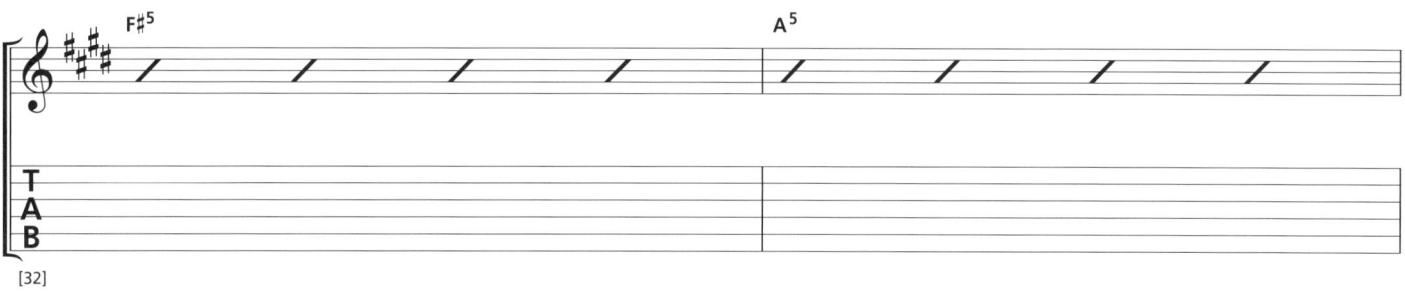

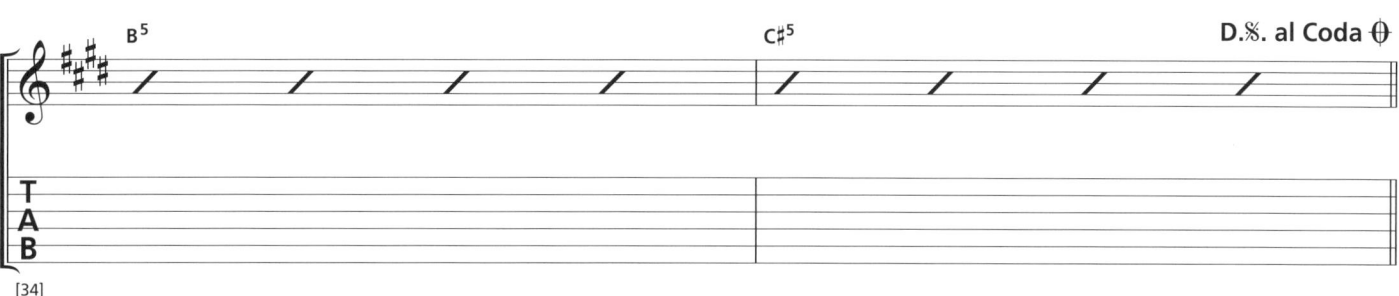

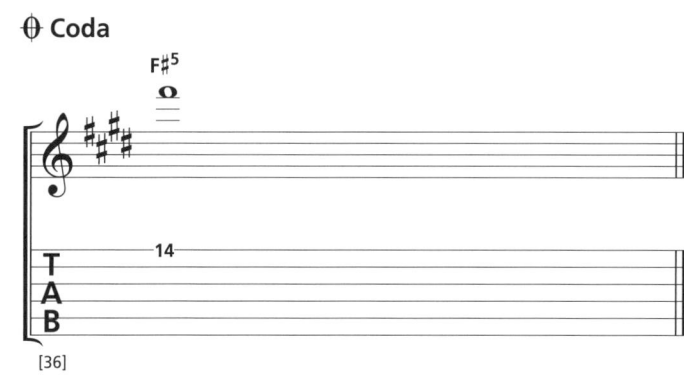

Walkthrough

Amp Settings

A smooth, high-gain distortion is a key part of this style's most famous tones. Although it's not an assessment requirement, adding delay, especially in the melody and lead sections, will help you achieve a more stylistic sound. A quarter-note delay with three repeats is ideal.

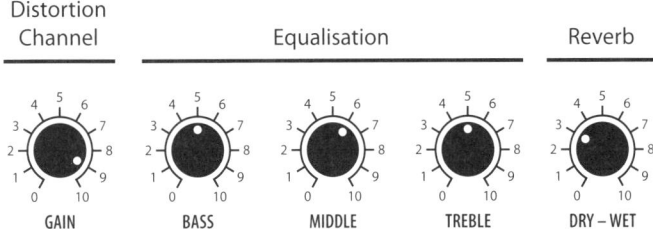

A Section (Measures 1–5)

The A section is a single-note riff built on a swung 16th feel. It uses pinched harmonics, slides and staccato notes.

Measures 1–5 | *Pinch harmonics*
Selecting the bridge pickup and using a high distortion setting will help here. Place your thumb close to the edge of the pick and dig into the strings. Both the pick and your thumb should strike the string. Pinch harmonics will only sound at certain 'node' points along the strings, so you'll need to experiment with your picking hand position.

B Section (Measures 6–13)

The B section is predominantly a single-string melody using fast slides, position shifts and bends.

Measures 6–11 | *Fast bends*
Repeatedly play the bends in this phrase slowly, paying close attention to the tuning. This will teach your fingers how far the string should be pushed up.

C Section (Measures 14–21)

The C section is a melody based on the F# dorian mode that 'answers' the riff played by the rest of the band.

Measure 21 | *Tapping*
The tapping pattern is based on a combination of shapes 1 and 2 of the minor pentatonic scale. Make solid contact with the tapping finger, then use a snapping motion towards the floor or ceiling to perform a clean pull-off to the next note.

Measures 21–22 | *Tapping to picking transition*
After you play the final tapped note of measure 21 and are performing the next three legato notes with your fretting hand move your picking hand back into position (i.e over the pickups) to play the next picked note (Fig. 1). Playing the tapped notes with your second finger will allow you to hold the pick normally throughout the phrase and transition smoothly back to picked notes.

D Section (Measures 22–29)

The D section is a variation of the B section. The melody is transposed by an octave and varied to include a descending run that ends with a pinched harmonic.

Measure 29 | *Crossing strings*
This challenging phrase requires a structured approach to both picking and fingering. Fig. 2 shows one possible option.

E & F Sections (Measures 14–36)

The E section is the guitar solo. Section F is a reprise of the C section with the opportunity to vary the notated part.

Measures 30–35 | *Guitar solo*
The F# blues, minor pentatonic scales can be used over the this solo. The F# dorian mode is an option and if you want a darker sound go for the F# natural minor scale.

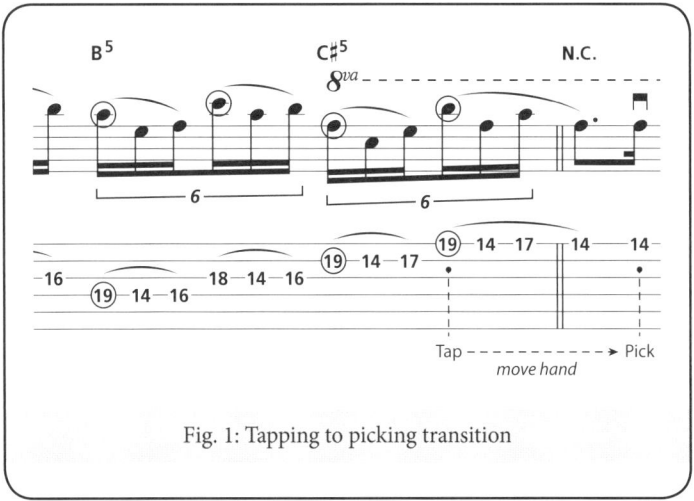

Fig. 1: Tapping to picking transition

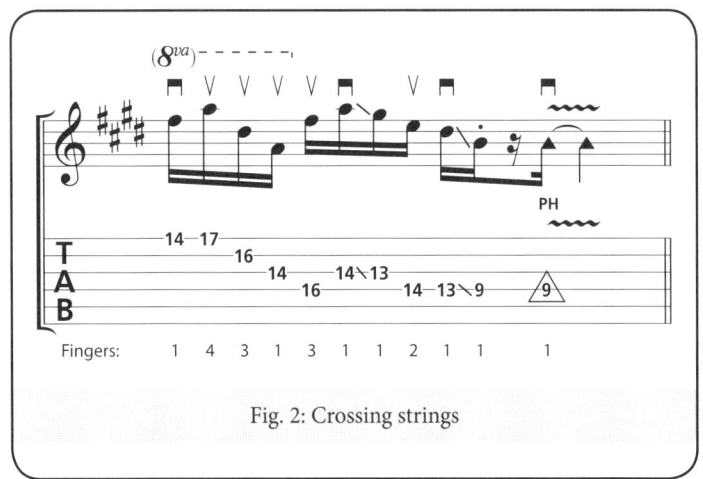

Fig. 2: Crossing strings

Blue Espresso

SONG TITLE: BLUE ESPRESSO
GENRE: BLUES
TEMPO: 116 BPM
KEY: B♭ (BLUES)

TECH FEATURES: BENDS
TRILLS
PARTIAL CHORDS

COMPOSER: DEIRDRE CARTWRIGHT

PERSONNEL: STUART RYAN (GTR)
HENRY THOMAS (BASS)
NOAM LEDERMAN (DRUMS)
ROSS STANLEY (KEYS)

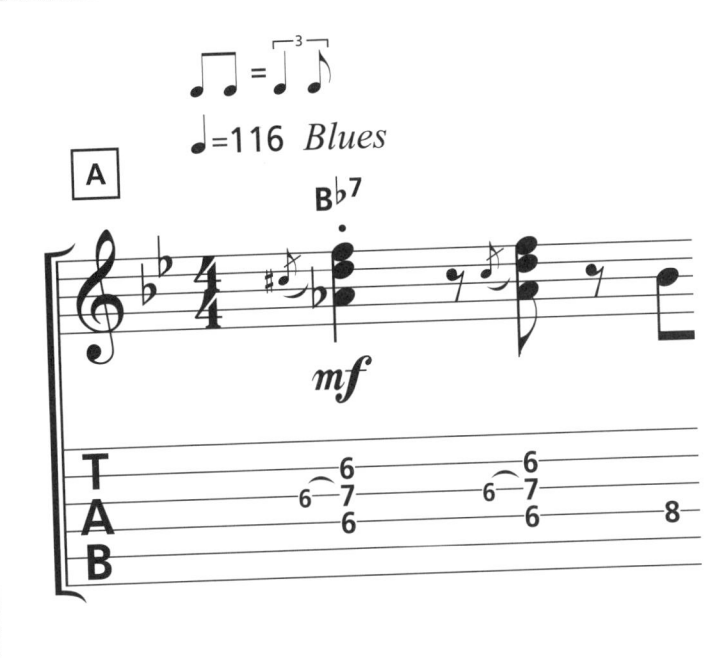

OVERVIEW

'Blue Espresso' is a composition in the style of blues legend B.B. King. The piece features some typical King style playing touches from the shuffle feel to the rapid, precise bends. A major feature of his guitar style is his fast vibrato and this particular piece is all about phrasing, timing and feel. The whole tone bends in particular are a technique that must be executed cleanly and to pitch. Notice on the rhythm guitar parts how you are playing partial chords, i.e., the chord has been condensed down to three notes rather than playing all six strings.

STYLE FOCUS

King is widely acknowledged as the godfather of electric blues guitar. His extensive influence is unparalleled and he has attained a level of popularity rarely seen in the world of blues for over six decades, reaching new generations with each new album or tour. His soulful playing is the epitome of taste and he is a master of space, choosing to play just one note where most players would fill the measure. In addition, this piece is played with a shuffle feel that is a key style in blues music. Make sure your playing is relaxed and get a good sense of how a shuffle should be played. This can be a real challenge when it comes to timing.

THE BIGGER PICTURE

Riley B 'Blues Boy' King was born on September 16, 1925, in Itta Bena, Mississippi. His professional career began with humble yet electrifying performances busking on street corners. It wasn't long before word spread of his talent on guitar and vocals, and of his songwriting abilities.

One of the hardest working guitarists in blues, King has released over 50 albums and has been known to perform up to 342 gigs in a year. He commands all forms of the blues, from the soul blues ballad hit 'The Thrill Is Gone' to the shuffle of 'Everyday I Have the Blues.' His powerful voice marries his guitar perfectly and has served to widen his appeal to an audience beyond that of guitarists.

RECOMMENDED LISTENING

King has many album credits to his name, but his 1965 release *Live At The Regal* is widely acknowledged as one of his best. In 2000, his album with Eric Clapton, *Riding With The King,* was critically acclaimed and won a Grammy award for Best Traditional Blues album. His instructional DVD, *Bluesmaster,* is also an invaluable resource for any guitarist aspiring to master this style.

Blue Espresso

Deirdre Cartwright

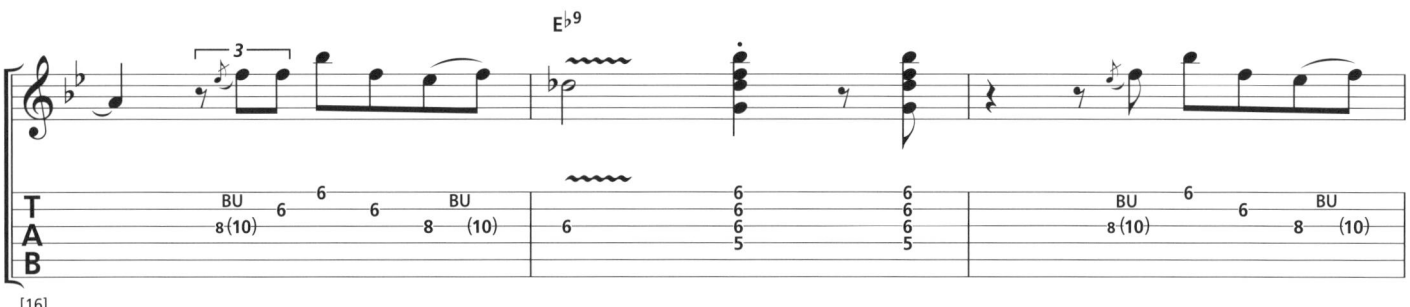

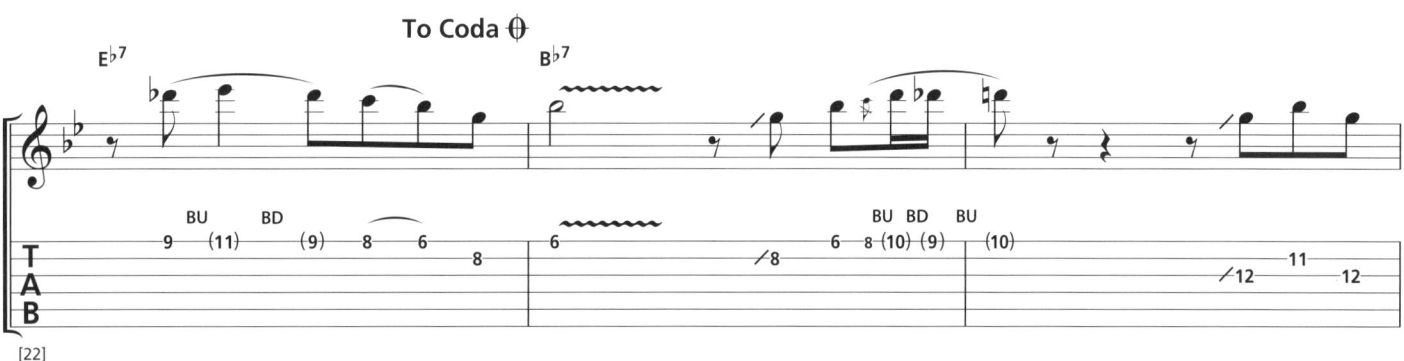
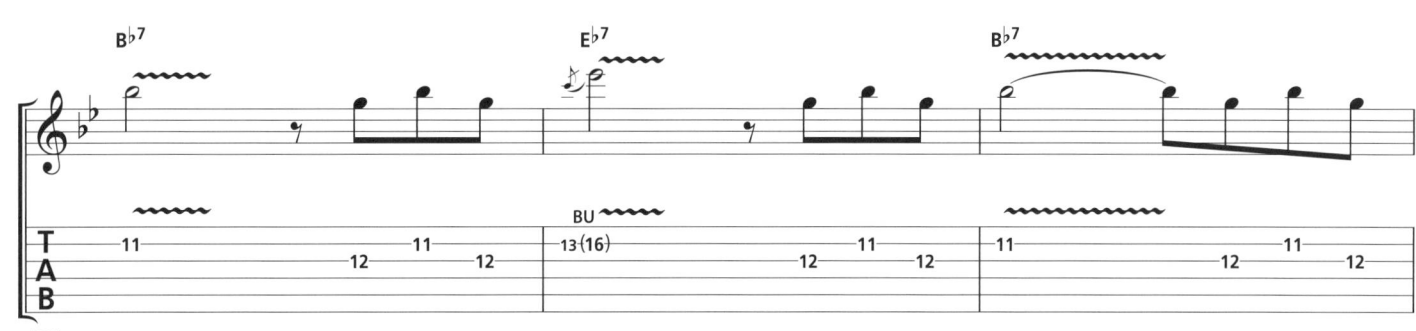

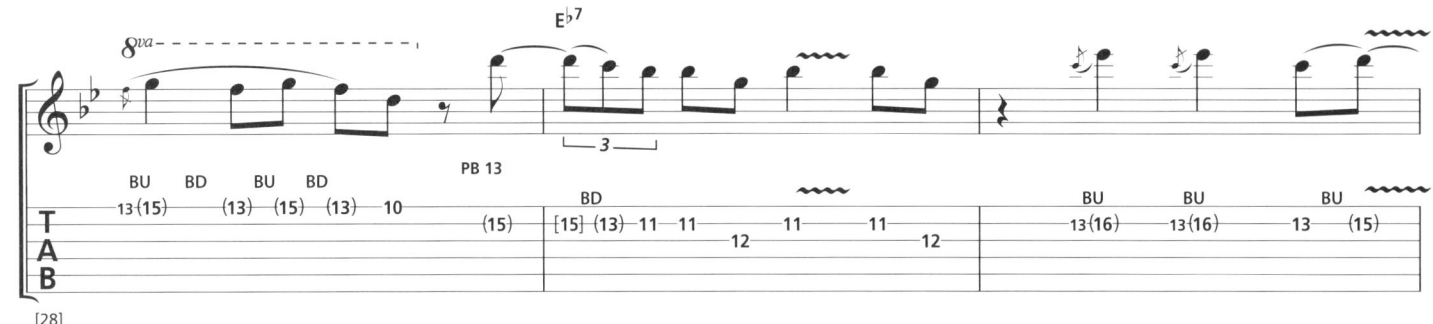
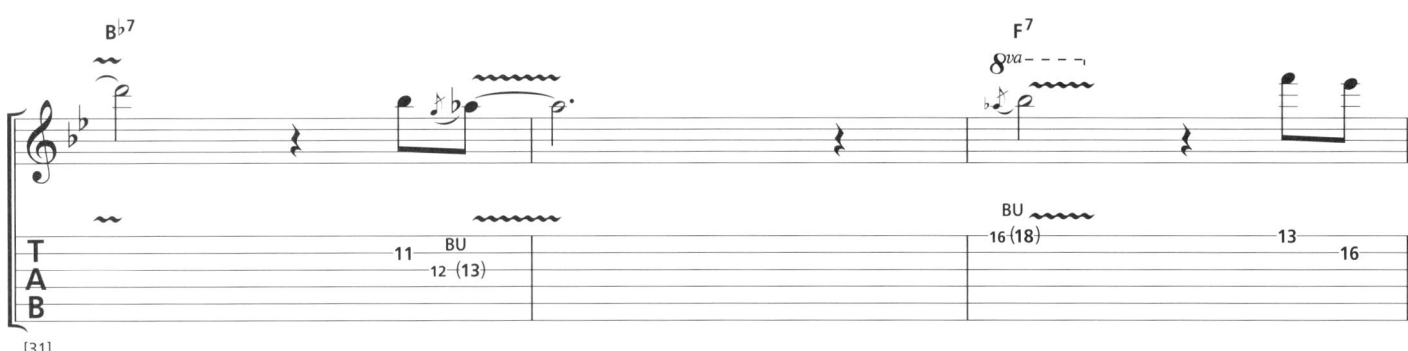
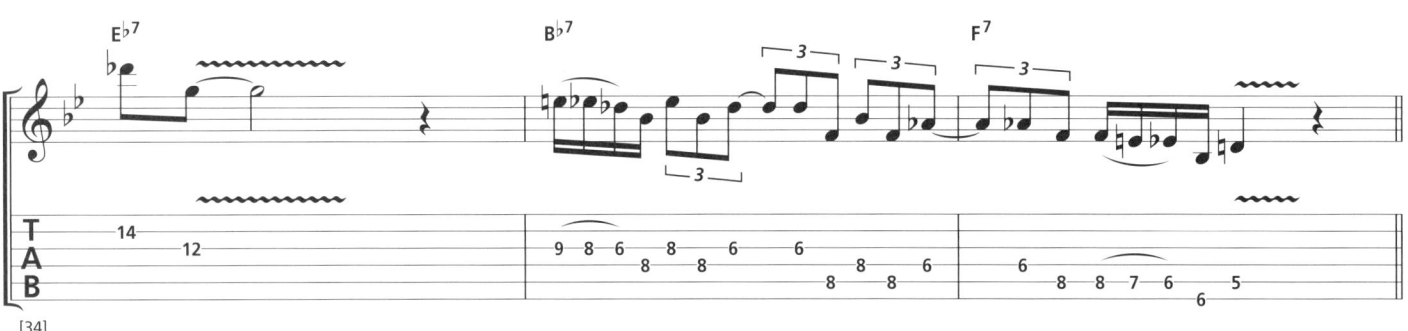
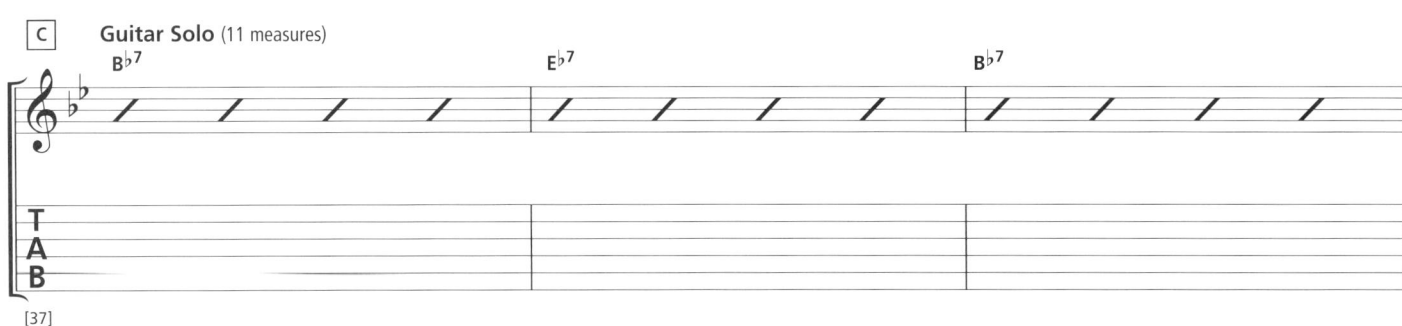

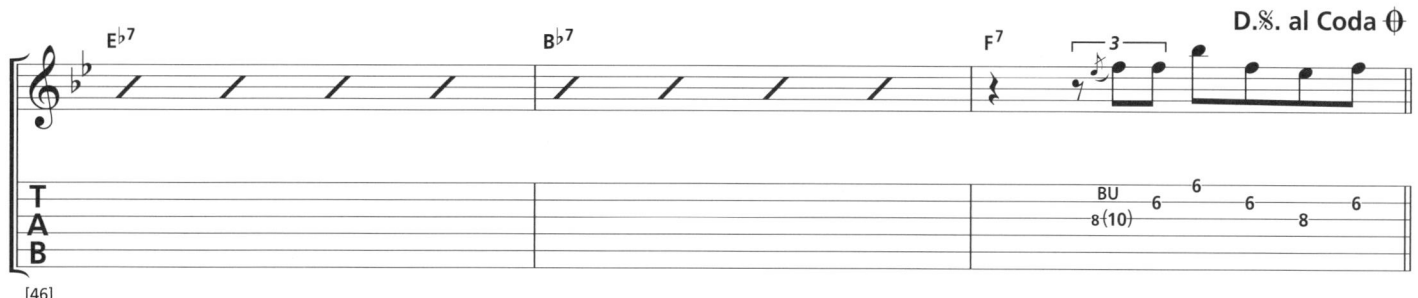
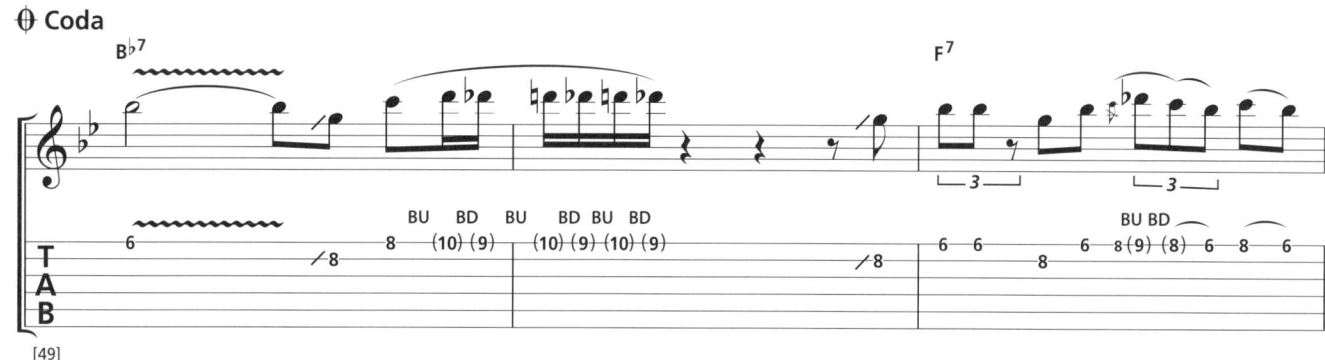
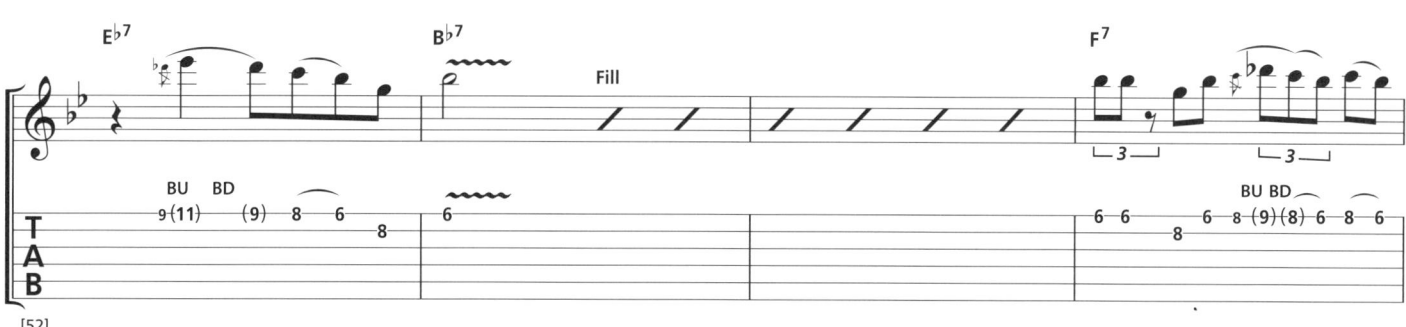

Walkthrough

Amp Settings

Aim for a clean, well-rounded tone with a fair amount of reverb. Reverb is not like the amp's other controls – even a reverb setting of 3 or 4 is considered quite high. BB King's tone is brighter than most people realise, so if you want to emulate this you may need to boost the treble.

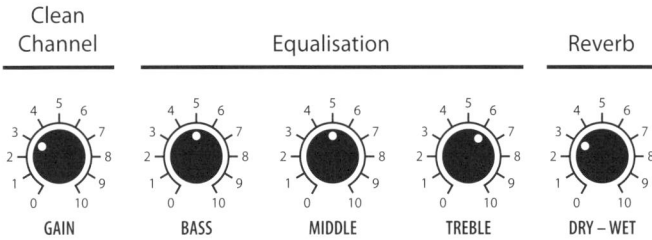

A Section (Measures 1–12)

The A section is a typical blues rhythm part that makes use of partial chords, grace notes and slides.

Measures 1–8 | *Grace notes*
Grace notes have no notational value so you should make sure the hammer-ons in this measure are sharp and snappy.

Measures 1–4 | *Fretting accuracy*
It's important that the last three notes of these measures do not ring into each other and sound like an arpeggiated chord. Play the B♭ with the tip of your third finger, 'roll' onto the flat of the same finger to play the double-stop then roll your finger back to play the B♭ again. This will separate the notes.

B Section (Measures 13–36)

The B section melody is made up of common blues techniques: string bends, trills, staccato chords and vibrato.

Measures 13–33 | *String bends*
The key to good string bends is making sure they reach the 'target note' (the note in brackets). A good exercise to help you develop your string bends is to play and hold the target note and then play the bend. Having the target note fresh in your memory will help you bend to the correct pitch (Fig. 1).

Measure 15 | *Trills*
Trills are indicated by the sign above the notation (Fig. 2). When you see this sign you should rapidly alternate between the two notes shown in brackets. In this case, the trill is articulated with hammer-ons and pull-offs.

Measure 28 | *Pre-bends*
A pre-bend is where the string is bent up to a specified pitch (the note you bend from is indicated above the notation) without being played. It is then picked and, usually, returned to its unbent position. If you have trouble playing this phrase, try playing the lick with regular bends instead of the pre-bend and release. Fig. 2 shows a breakdown of how you can practice this.

C Section (Measures 37–48)

Here you can improvise over a 12-bar blues progression.

Measures 37–48 | *Guitar solo*
While the minor pentatonic and blues scales are obvious choices to solo with, there are several other more advanced options you may want to consider. One option is to use the relevant mixolydian mode over each chord. Some players choose to mix this mode with the blues scale. Another option is to use the appropriate dominant ^{7} arpeggios to outline the chord changes.

D Section (Measures 13–58)

This is a reprise of the B section where you must vary the melody before jumping to the *Coda* to close the piece.

Measures 53–54 | *Fill*
You should create your own fill here. Aside from making sure it is appropriate stylistically, the fill should flow seamlessly from and into the notated parts.

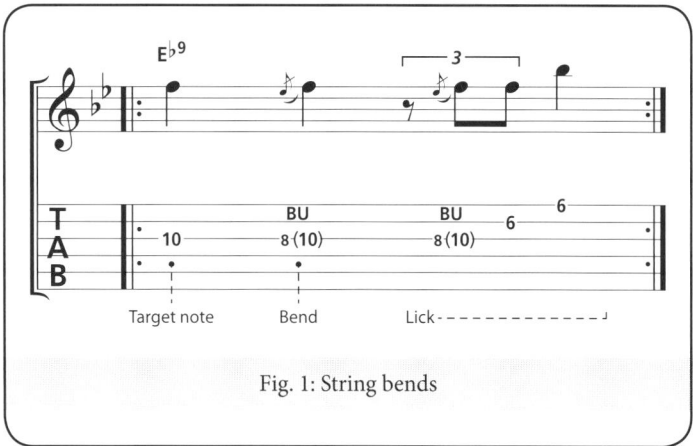

Fig. 1: String bends

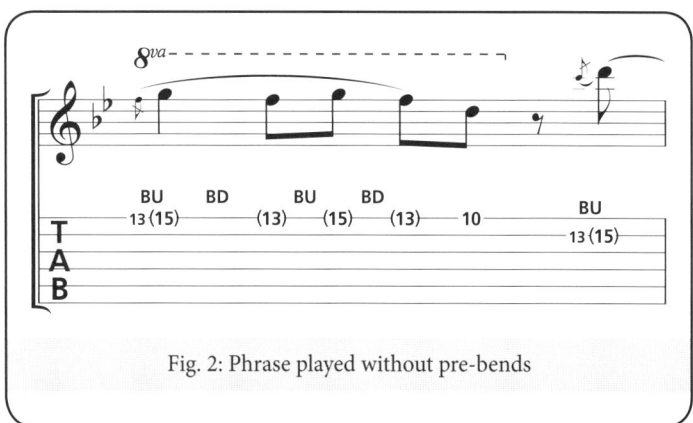

Fig. 2: Phrase played without pre-bends

Cranial Contraption

SONG TITLE: CRANIAL CONTRAPTION
GENRE: METAL
TEMPO: 105 BPM
KEY: E MINOR

TECH FEATURES: ARPEGGIATED CHORDS
SINGLE-NOTE RIFFS
NATURAL HARMONICS

COMPOSER: CHARLIE GRIFFITHS

PERSONNEL: CHARLIE GRIFFITHS (GTR)
DAVE MARKS (BASS)
JASON BOWLD (DRUMS)

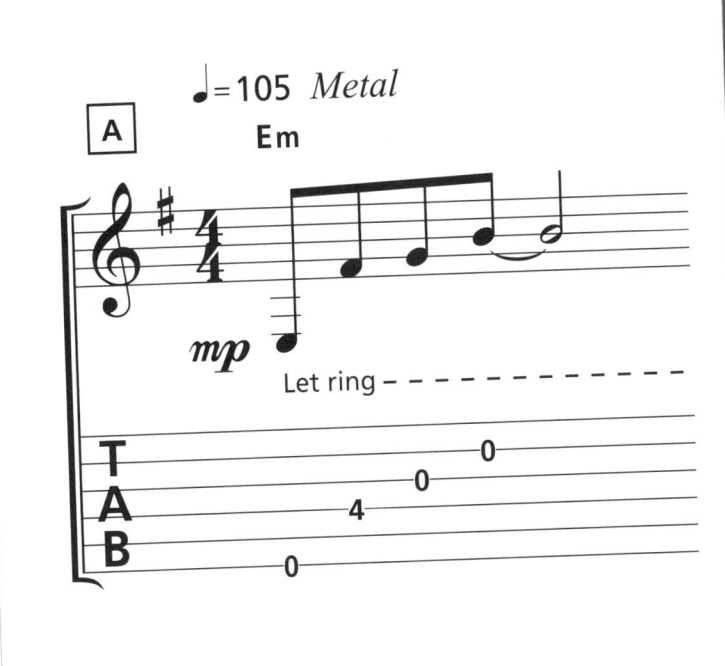

OVERVIEW

'Cranial Contraption' is a thrash/metalcore track that brings to mind Machine Head, Shadows Fall, Disturbed and Slipknot. The intro chord arrangement is played with a clean sound and the intensity builds with the octave melody, which is played with distortion. So too are the verse and breakdown sections that feature heavy riffs with contrasting low notes and high natural harmonics.

STYLE FOCUS

Metalcore is a branch of thrash metal that relies on intense playing and dark, distorted riffs that are locked in rhythmically with the bass and drums, particularly in the verse sections. By contrast, the choruses are usually more melodic. There is almost always a stomping breakdown section later in the song. The minor scales aeolian (natural minor), phrygian and harmonic minor are used with a focus on single note and powerchord riffing.

THE BIGGER PICTURE

The roots of this sub genre go back to the early 1990s when bands like Sepultura and Machine Head began to cross their Slayer and Metallica influenced sounds with the edginess and intense delivery of punk and hardcore bands like Black Flag and Misfits.

This style of metal grew throughout the 1990s and 2000s with bands including Hatebreed, Shadows Fall and Killswitch Engage who worked with strong melodic hooks. Meanwhile, The Dillinger Escape Plan infused the style with more technical playing and aggressive rap-like vocals. In 1999, Slipknot released their self-titled debut and popularised the style by maintaining a great balance between each of those elements. The genre is still growing thanks to bands Bullet For My Valentine, As I Lay Dying, The Devil Wears Prada and others.

RECOMMENDED LISTENING

Sepultura's *Chaos A.D.* (1993) was perhaps the first album to cross thrash with industrial and hardcore, while Machine Head's *Burn My Eyes* (1994) influenced many metal and hardcore bands, as did Slipknot's debut. Sweden's Soilwork are great musicians and demonstrate strong melodic hooks on *Stabbing The Drama* (2005). Mathcore is the latest sub genre to have evolved from metalcore and The Dillinger Escape Plan's *Ire Works* (2007) demonstrates how far this style has come from its ancestor.

Cranial Contraption

Charlie Griffiths

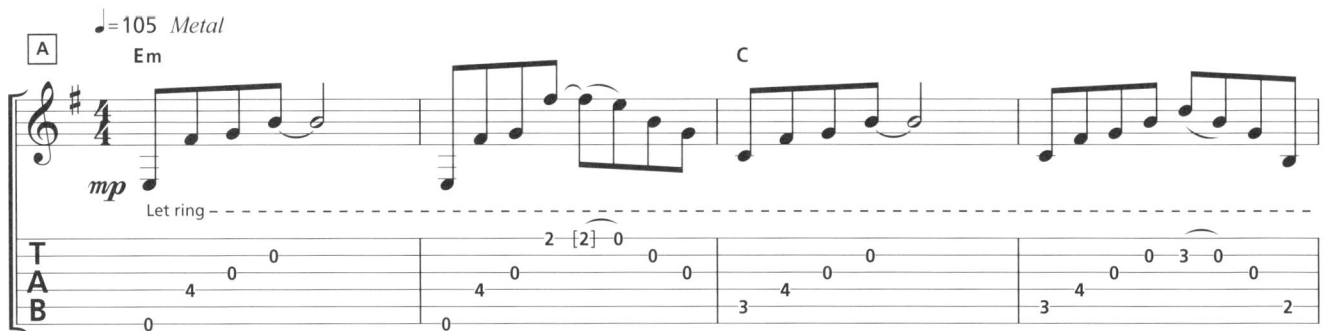
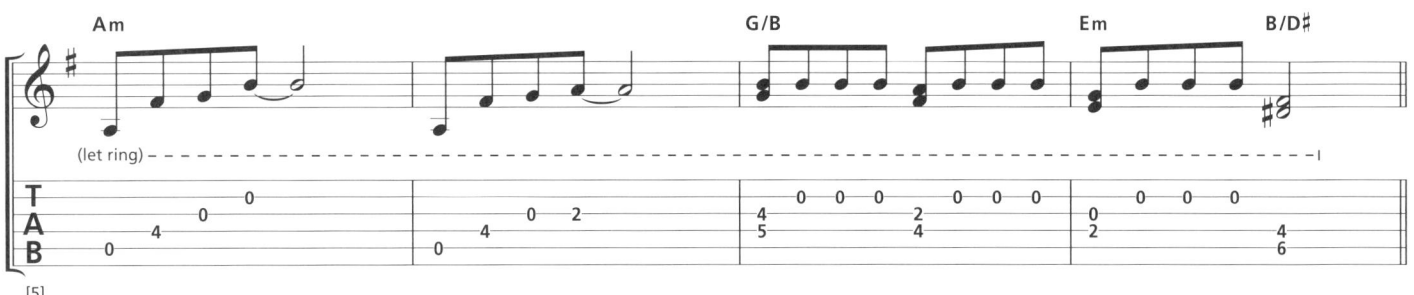

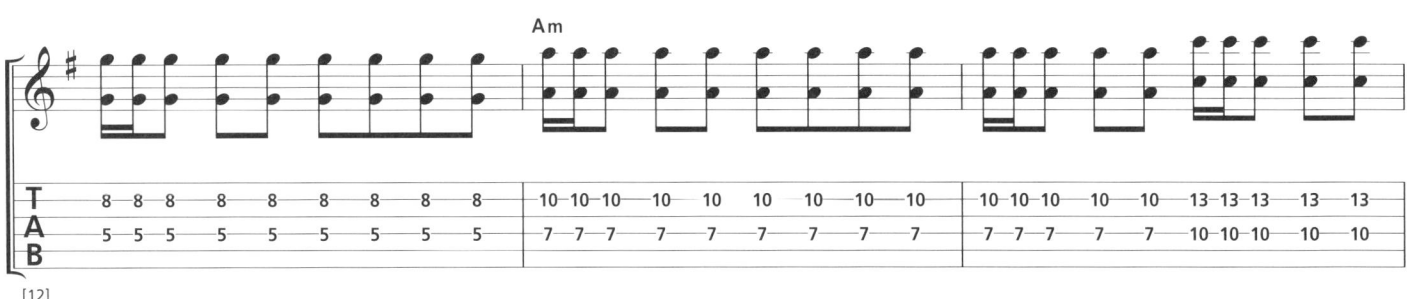
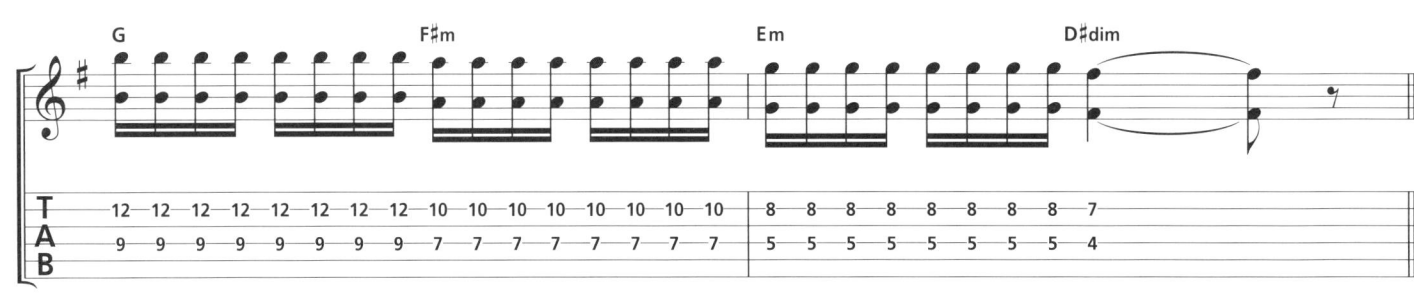

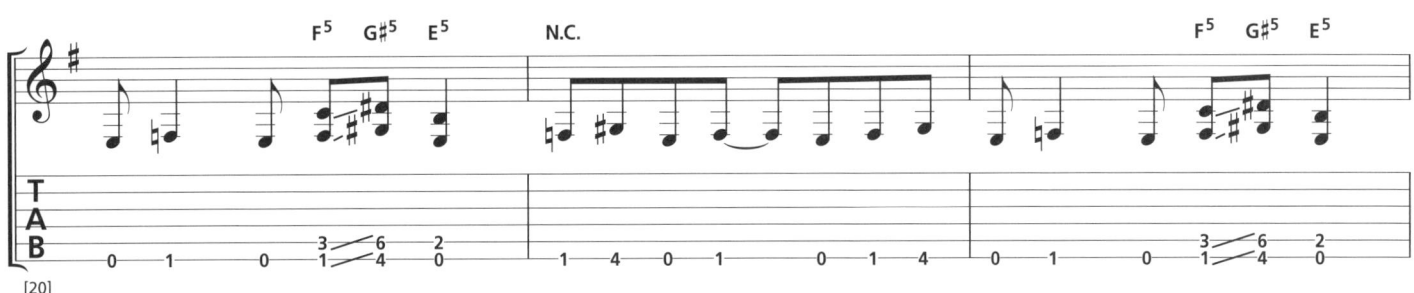
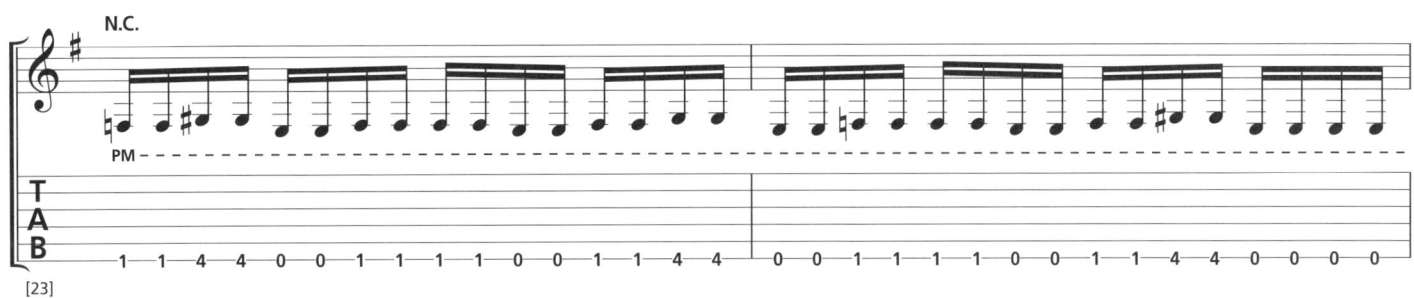
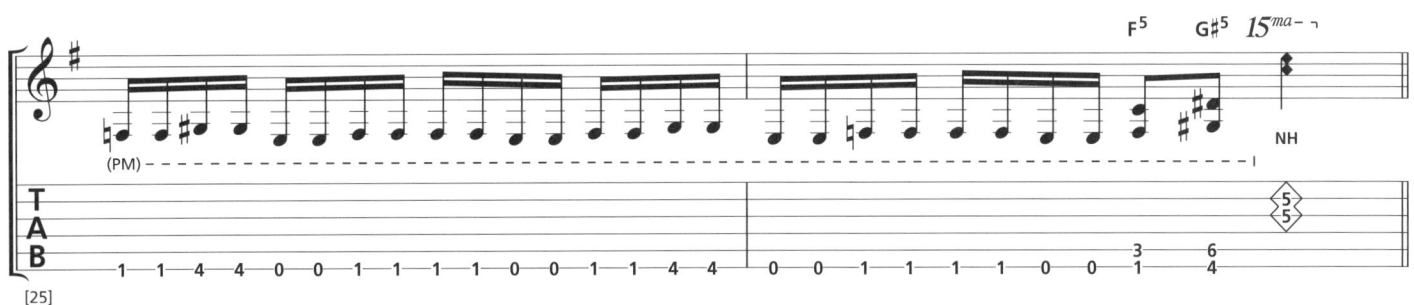

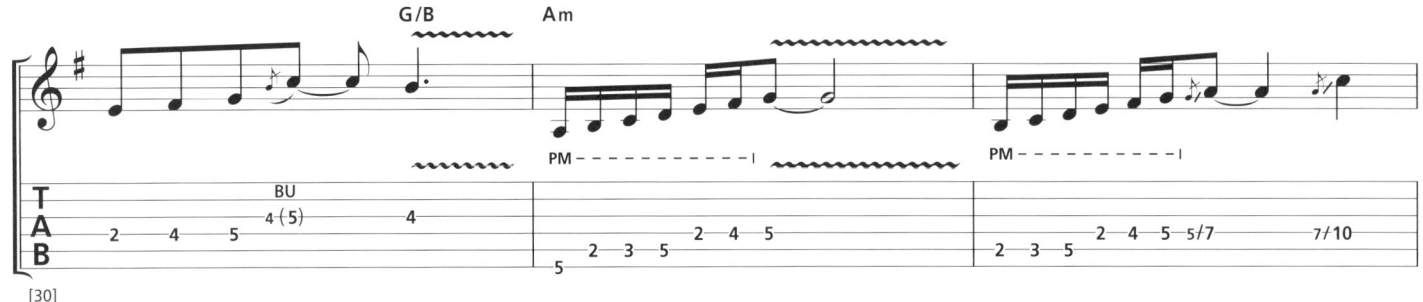

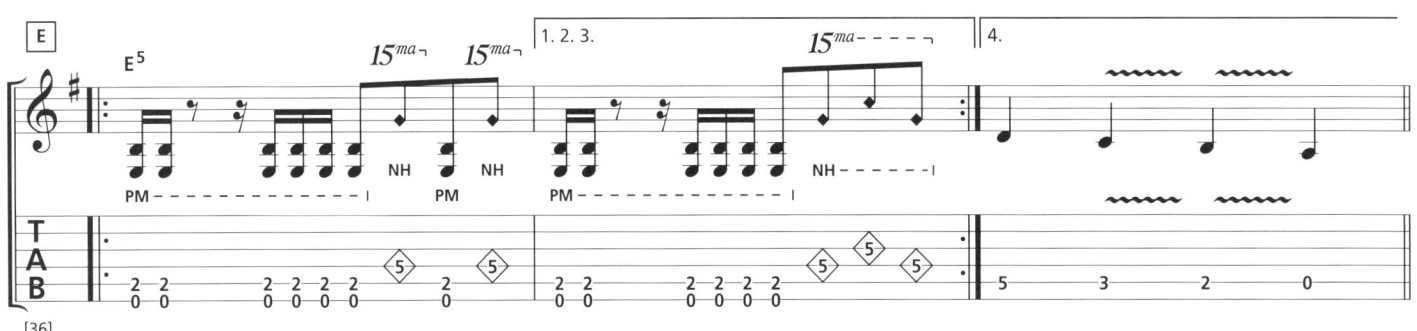
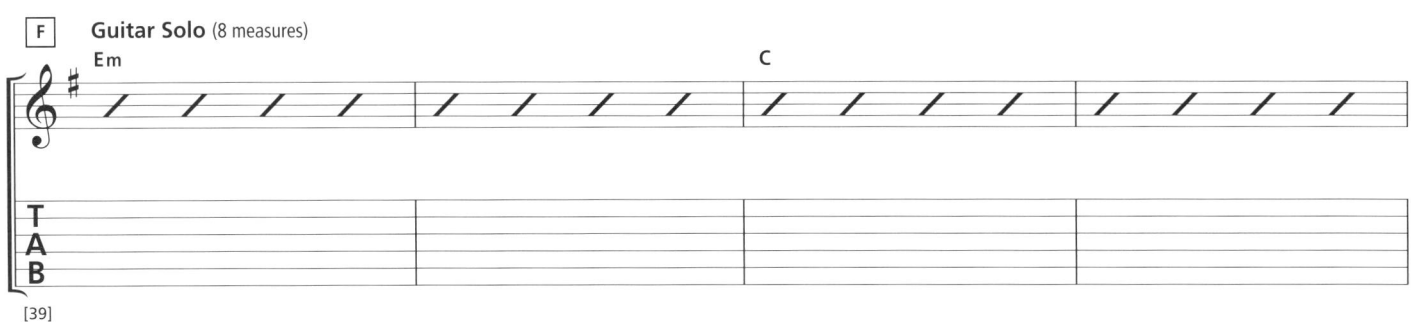
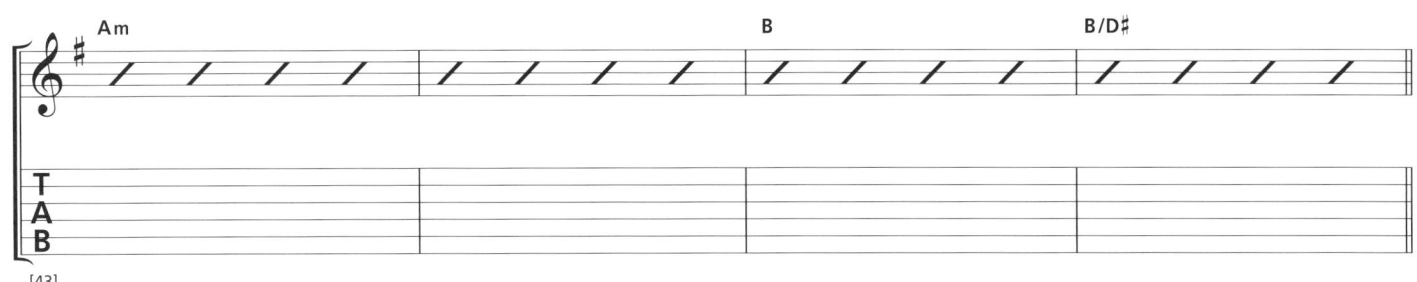

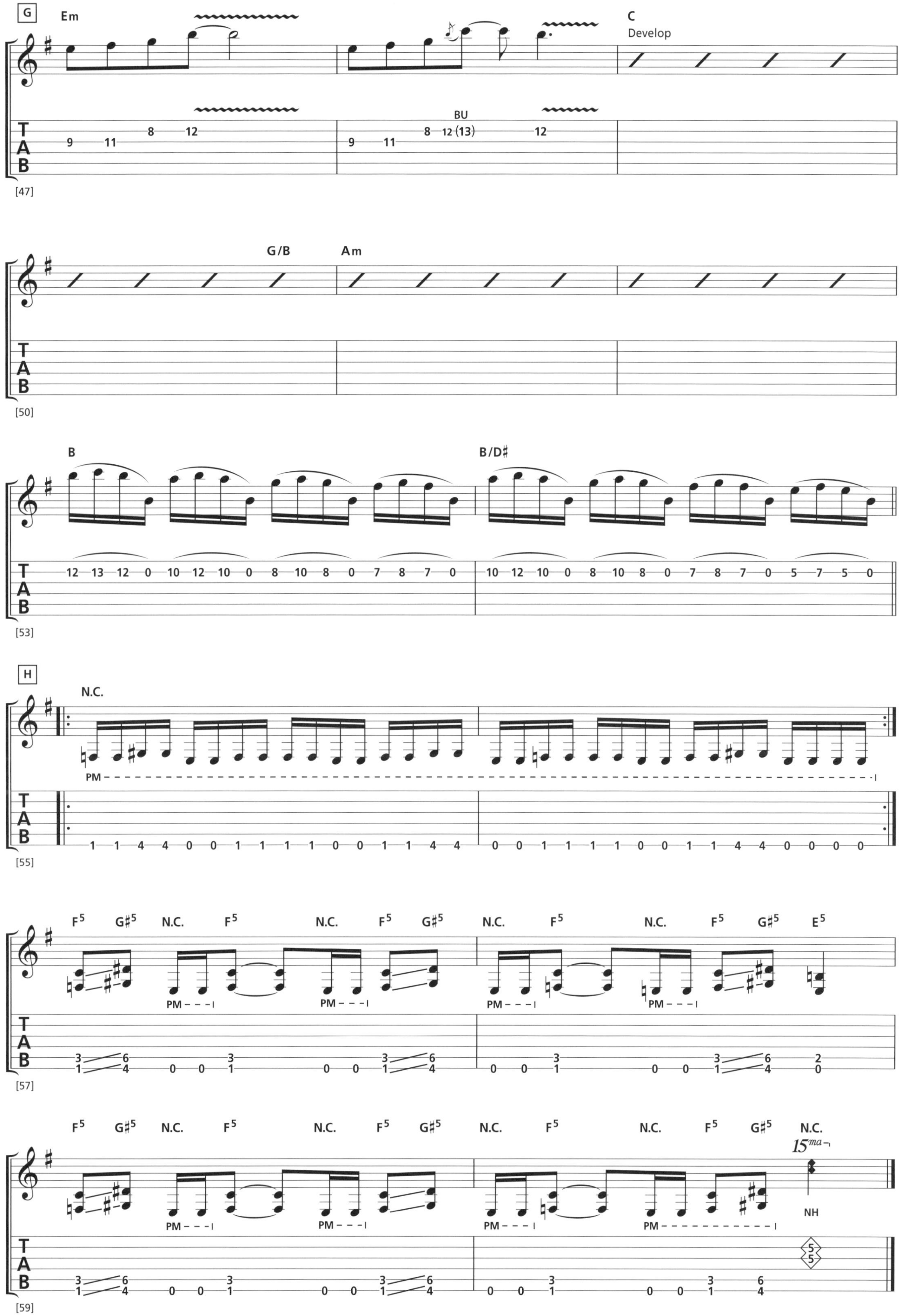
G
Em
C
Develop
BU
[47]
G/B
Am
[50]
B
B/D♯
[53]
H
N.C.
PM
[55]
F5 G♯5 N.C. F5 N.C. F5 G♯5 N.C. F5 N.C. F5 G♯5 E5
PM
[57]
F5 G♯5 N.C. F5 N.C. F5 G♯5 N.C. F5 N.C. F5 G♯5 N.C.
15ma
NH
PM
[59]

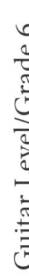

Walkthrough

Amp Settings
The metal guitar tone consists of two key elements: a modern high-gain distortion and a scooped tone. A scooped tone is achieved by boosting the treble and bass controls and cutting or 'scooping out' the middle. When combined with the extreme distortion this creates a heavy, aggressive tone.

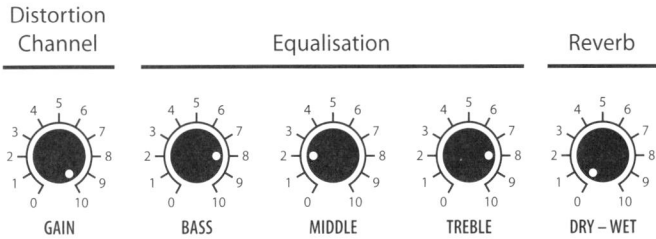

A and B Sections (Measures 1–16)
The A section is based on arpeggiated open chords. While the part uses some exotic extensions, the chord symbols reflect the song's overall harmony. The B section is based exclusively on octaves played on the D and B strings.

Measures 1–8 | *Fretting accuracy*
Play the fretted notes with the tips of your fingers so that you can arch your fingers over the open strings. This will stop the strings from being muted and allow them to ring out once they have been played and you are moving on to the next chord.

Measure 8 | *Changing tones*
There is a two-beat gap from striking the last note of the A section and the start of the B section. Use this time to prepare to change from a clean to a distorted tone before you play the first note of the B section.

C Section (Measures 17–26)
This heavy riff is first played in eighth notes, followed by a variation played in 16th notes. Natural harmonics are used to create a dramatic contrast to the low, heavy riffs.

Measure 18 | *Natural harmonics*
These natural harmonics at the 5th fret require quick position shifts, so your finger placements need to be more accurate than those of harmonics found at other frets (Fig. 1).

Measures 23–26 | *Fast rhythm parts*
The key to playing heavy parts at this speed is to use a relaxed picking action minimising excess motion – your pick should only travel a small amount past the string.

D Section (Measures 27–35)
The D section is a melodic part that uses string bends and vibrato as well as fast, alternate picked lines.

Measures 29–34 | *Alternate picking*
These runs should be played using alternate picking (Fig. 2). They are challenging and will take some practice to master. Start slowly, working with a metronome, and concentrate on accuracy rather than speed.

E & F Sections (Measures 36–46)
The E section is a low, choppy riff using natural harmonics to create contrast. The F section is the guitar solo.

Measures 39–46 | *Scale choices*
The E harmonic minor scale can be used for the whole solo. Some people find this scale's distinctive sound too exotic to be used all the time, so you may prefer to use the minor pentatonic, blues or natural minor scales until measure 45 where the D♯ in the harmonic minor is required for the B chord.

G & H Sections (Measures 47–60)
The G section is a variation of the D section, where you must develop the original melody. The H section consists of variations of the C section.

Measures 47–52 | *Developing a part*
Develop the part played in measures 47–48. Some ways to achieve this are to vary the rhythm, note choices or articulations.

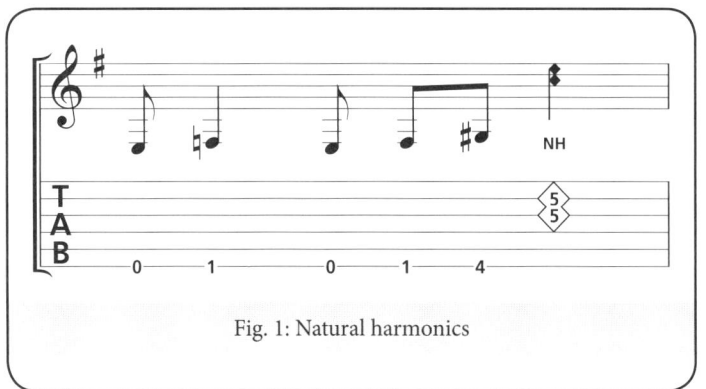

Fig. 1: Natural harmonics

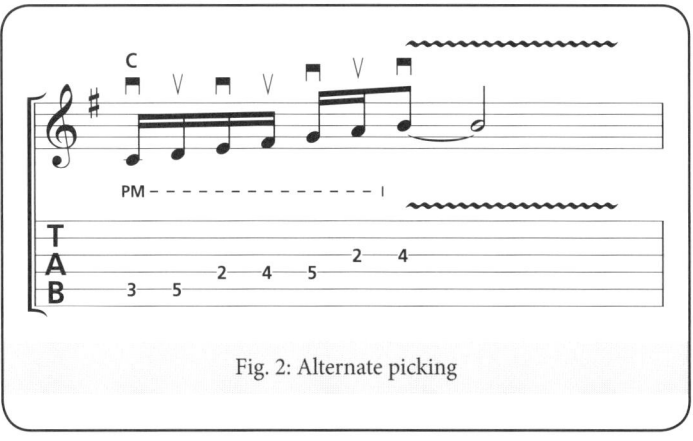

Fig. 2: Alternate picking

Favela

SONG TITLE: FAVELA
GENRE: SAMBA
TEMPO: 109 BPM
KEY: A MINOR

TECH FEATURES: SYNCOPATION

COMPOSER: NOAM LEDERMAN

PERSONNEL: NOAM LEDERMAN (DRUMS)
HENRY THOMAS (BASS)
STUART RYAN (GTR)
KISHON KHAN (KEYS)
FERGUS GERRAND (PERC)
RICHARD PARDY (SAX)
STEVE WALKER (TRUMPET)
ANDY CROMPTON (TROMBONE)

OVERVIEW

'Favela' is a Brazilian samba flavoured track boasting octave melodies, syncopation, slides and double-stops among its techniques.

STYLE FOCUS

'Favela' is a mixture of bossa nova and tropicália. The acoustic guitar is a prominent feature of bossa nova, usually played fingerstyle. However, bossa nova can be played with electric and jazz techniques; slides and octave melodies are commonly used. Tropicália was inspired by rock'n'roll as much as Rio De Janeiro, so distorted riffs are not unheard of.

THE BIGGER PICTURE

Samba is the rhythmic, syncopated music of Brazil with roots in the country's African culture. The first samba record is believed to be 'Pelo Telefone', which was released in 1917 and gave the style its first significant exposure outside of the favelas (slums). It made such an impression that, in the 1930s, the nationalist dictatorship in power supported its promotion to the national music of Brazil.

Early samba records relied on drums and percussion (think of the sound of Rio De Janeiro's carnival marching bands) and were revered for their raw energy rather than musical sophistication. However, this changed in the 1950s when João Gilberto and Antonio Carlos Jobim, among others, brought in supple melodies and jazz influenced harmonies. This new style or 'bossa nova' exposed Brazilian music to the world. Its best-known song is 'The Girl From Ipanema', which was translated into English and performed by stars including Frank Sinatra.

Bossa nova's sense of sophistication and restraint made it ideal for hotel lounges and Las Vegas theatres, but new left-wing politics were afoot in Brazil in the late 1960s. The sounds and sentiment of the favelas erupted through the music of Chico Buarque, Caetano Veloso and Os Mutantes, a molten fusion of samba, rock, funk and jazz. Its name was 'Tropicália' and it remains popular to this day.

RECOMMENDED LISTENING

Gilberto's *Chega de Saudade* (1959) is a classic bossa nova record. To hear how Brazilian music changed in the 1960s, listen to the albums *Caetano Veloso* (1969) and Buarque's *Construção* (1971).

Favela

Noam Lederman

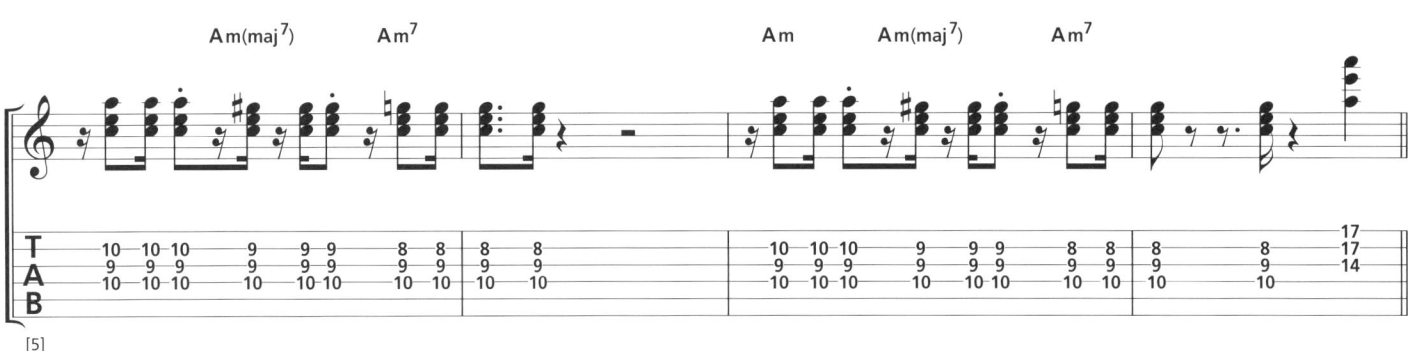
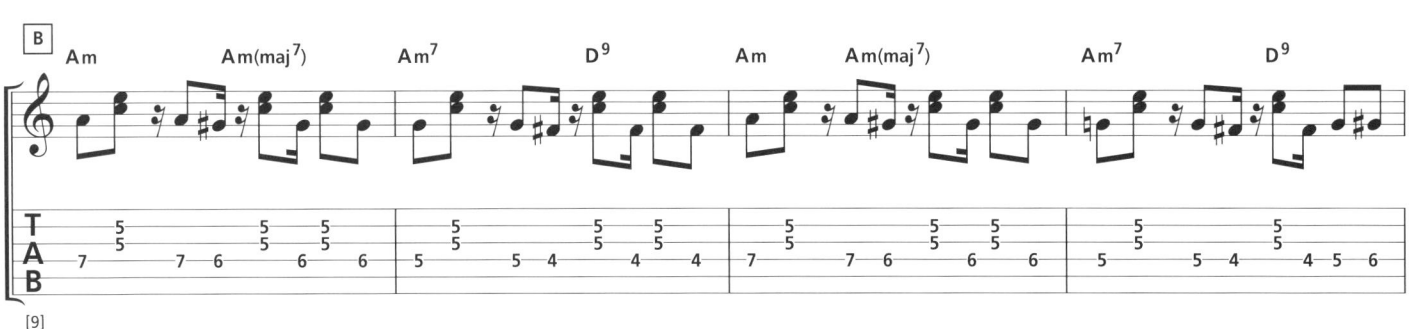
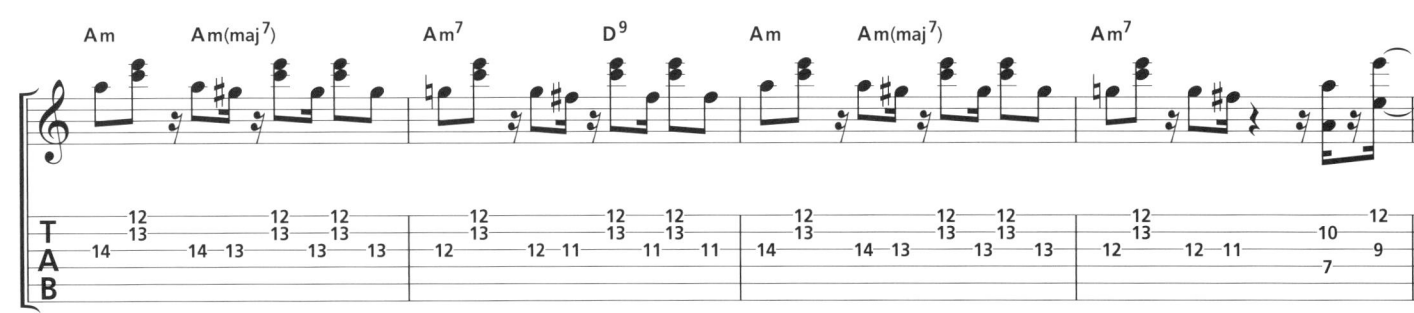

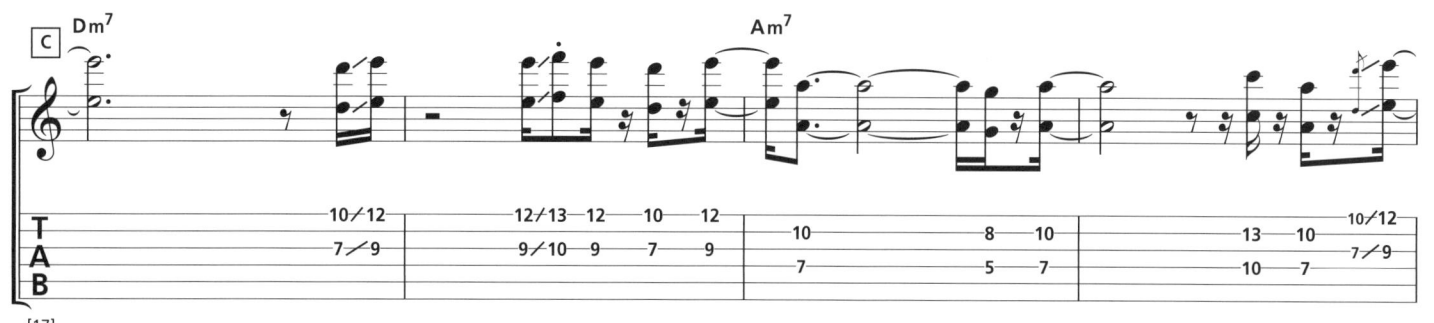
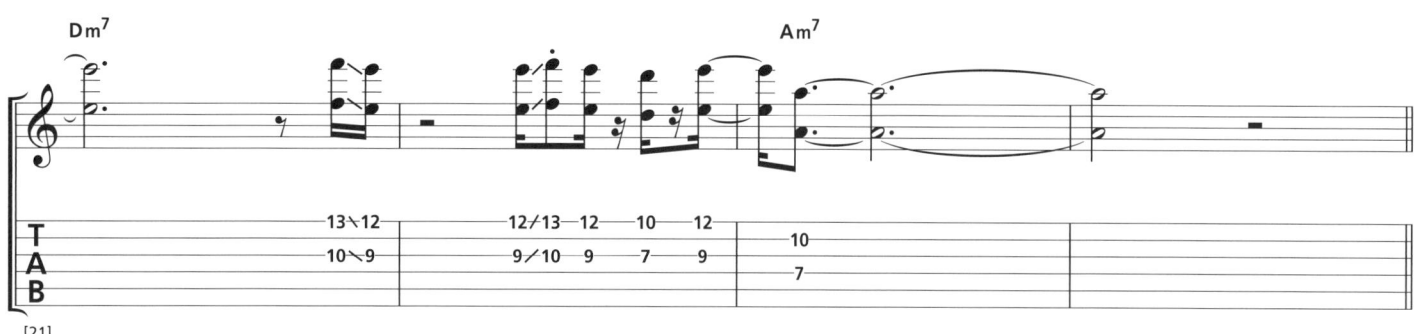
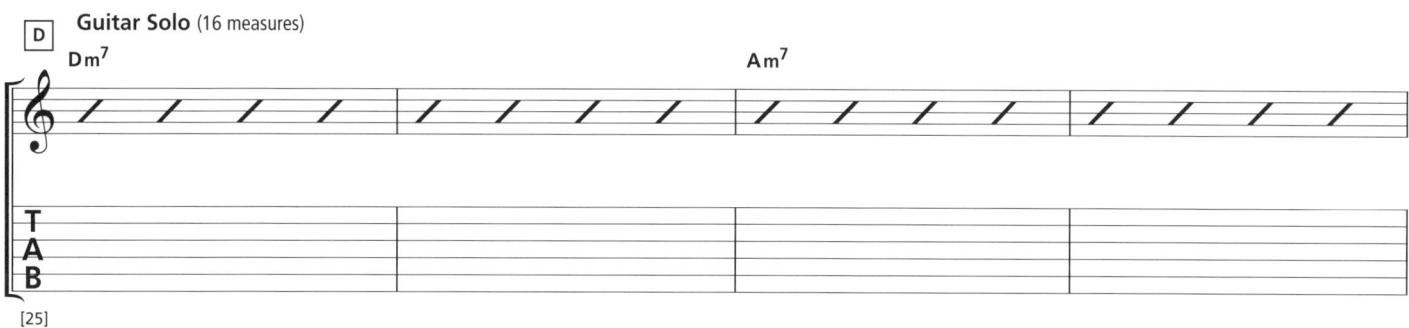
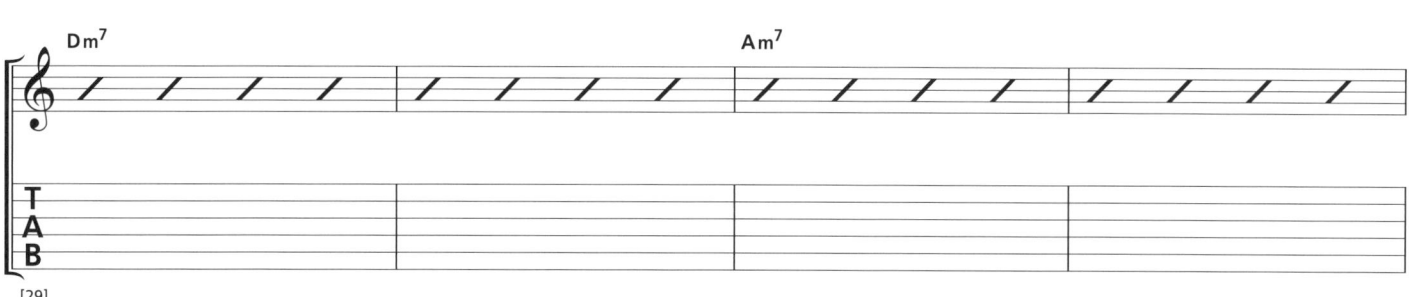
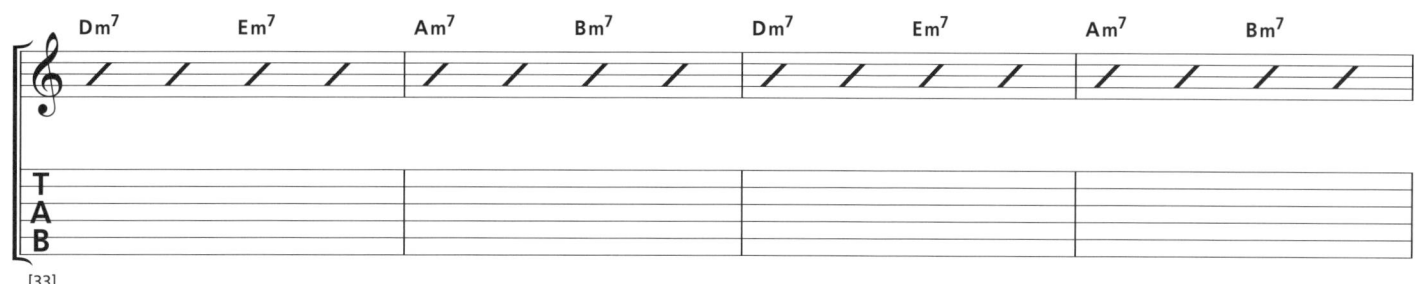

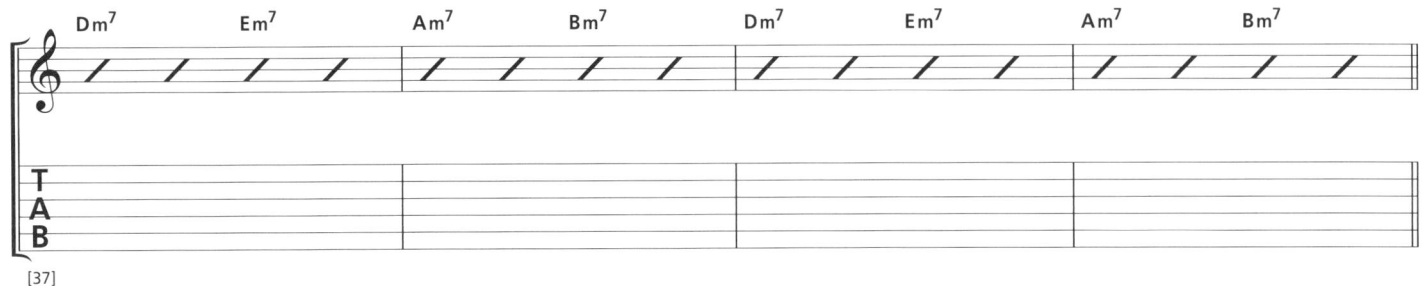
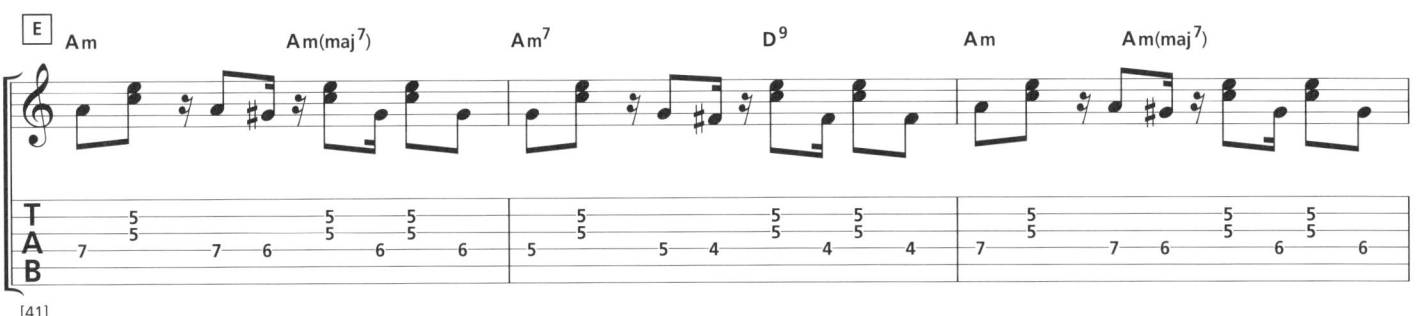
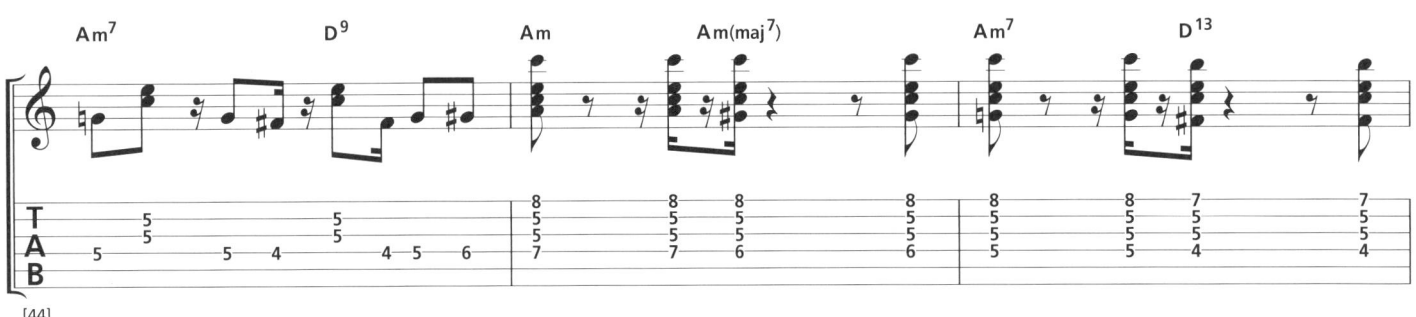
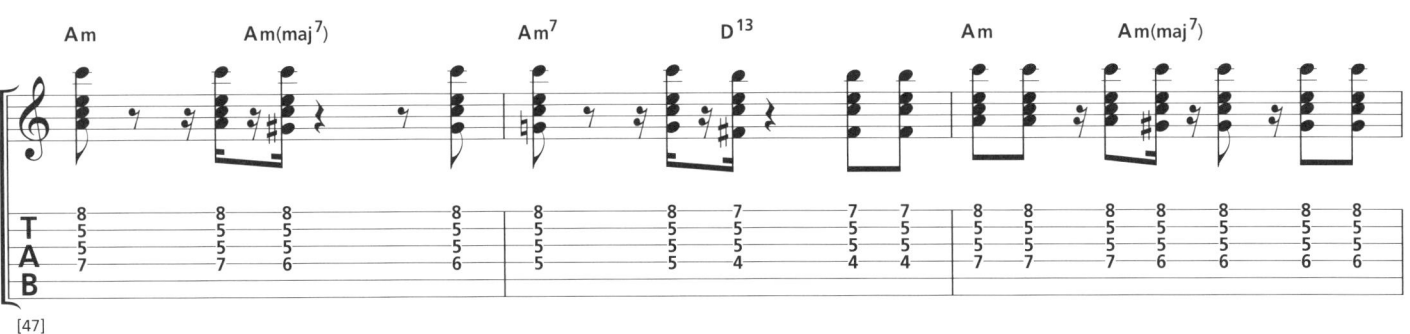
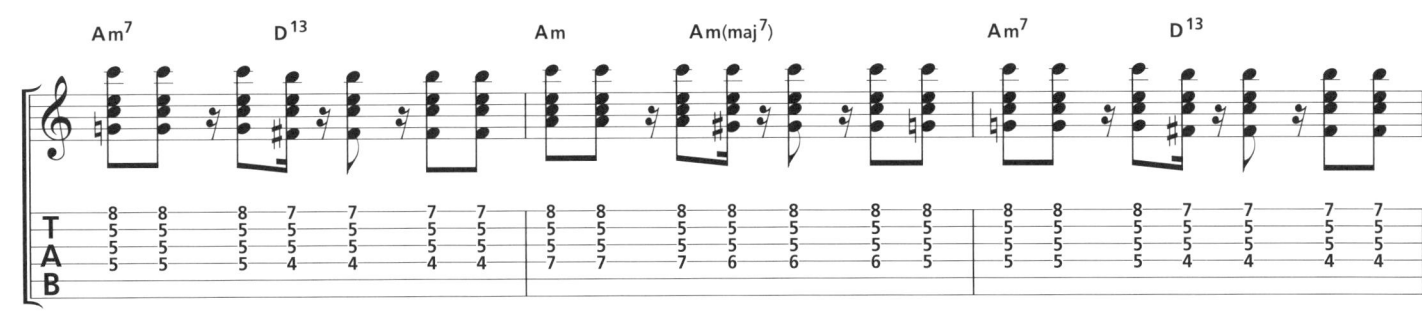

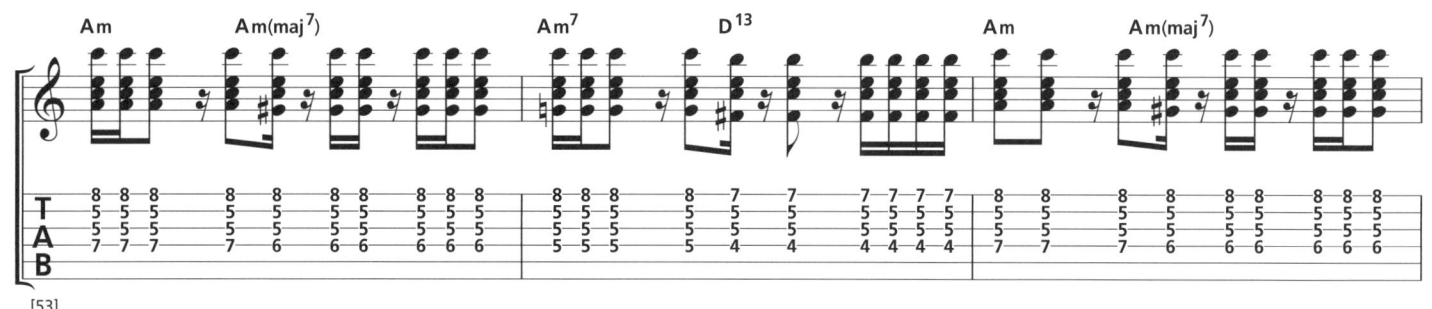
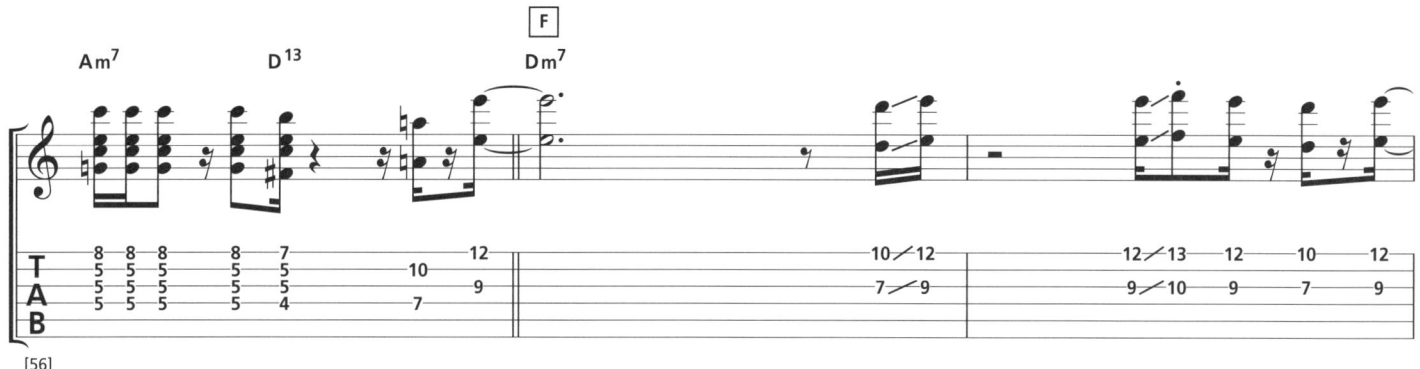
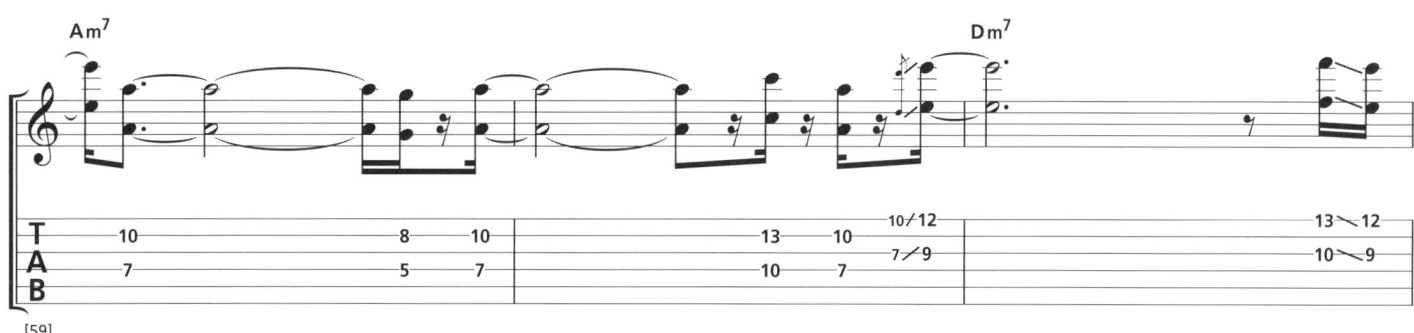
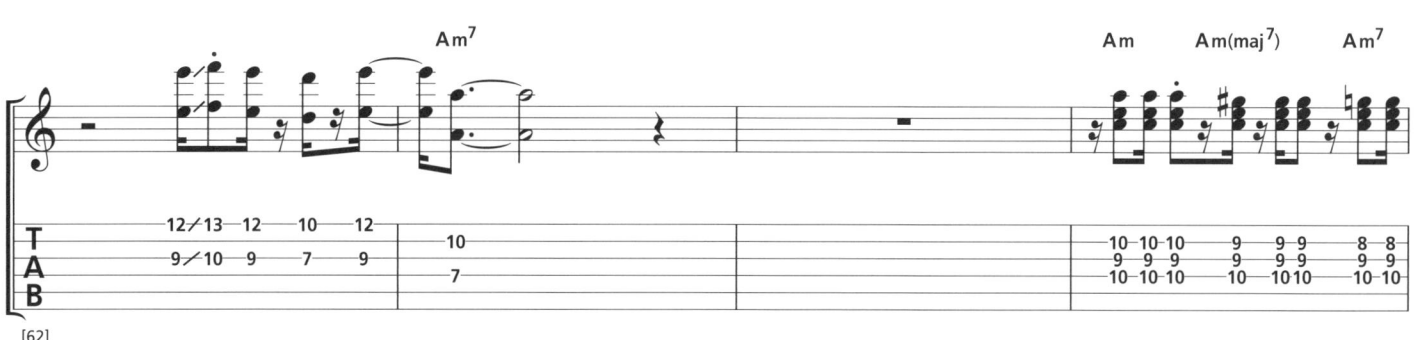
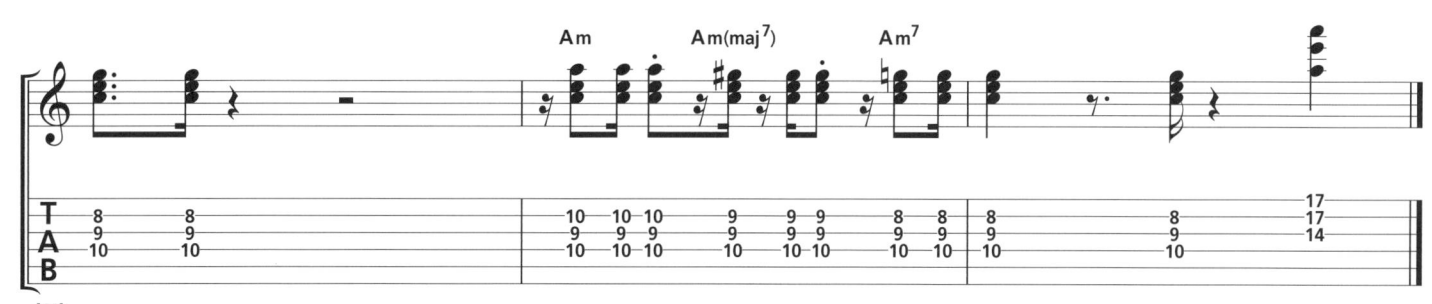

Walkthrough

Amp Settings

For this song you need a clean, full and warm tone. Using your guitar's neck pickup will help with this. Boost the bass (but don't let the sound become to muddy) and roll off the middle and treble if you feel the tone is too harsh.

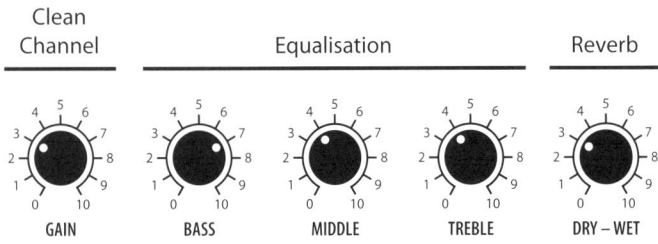

A Section (Measures 1–8)
The A section starts with a single-note melody then moves into a heavily syncopated chordal part with a chromatically descending line.

Measures 5–8 | *Syncopated rhythms*
This syncopated rhythm will take some preparation to play well. Work slowly through the rhythm while counting 16th notes ("1 e & a 2 e & a 3 e & a 4 e & a") (Fig. 1). You should work on feeling the rhythm rather than counting it to help your performance sound more convincing. A 16th-note strumming pattern will help you maintain the pulse through the numerous syncopated rhythms.

B Section (Measures 9–16)
The descending line from the A section is moved down an octave and a new rhythm is introduced.

Measures 9–16 | *Imitating a piano part*
It is possible to play this part using a pick, however the pianist plays the C and E double-stops simultaneously while a guitarist using a pick will play them so that they are slightly staggered. Fingerpicking or hybrid picking will allow you to play these two notes as the piano does to enhance the feel.

C Section (Measures 17–24)
This octave melody uses slides and quick position shifts.

Measures 17–24 | *Sliding octaves*
Approach sliding octaves in the same way as powerchords and barre chords: lock your fingers in position and move the fretting hand as a unit rather than dealing with individual finger placement. The difficulty of sliding octaves is that you must maintain pressure on the strings to keep the notes ringing. You should feel as if you are pushing into the fretboard as well as sliding up or down to a new fret.

D Section (Measures 25–40)
The D section is the guitar solo. The chord progression you will solo over is composed entirely of minor chords.

Measures 25–40 | *Guitar solo*
The four minor chords in the second half can be played in many ways. The main challenge is dealing with the F in the Dm^7 chord and the F♯ in the Bm^7 chord. You could treat the first measure as A natural minor and the second as A dorian, or bypass the F or F♯ and use the minor pentatonic or blues scales. These scales may limit your note choices, however.

E & F Sections (Measures 41–68)
The E section starts with a reprise of the B section then outlines the chord progression using syncopated strumming. The F section is a reprise of parts found earlier in the piece.

Measures 45–56 | *16th-note strumming*
Sixteenth-note strumming where the picking hand strums four times for every beat of the measure can aid fluency. The pick does not strike the string four times per beat – some of these will be ghost strums (Fig. 2).

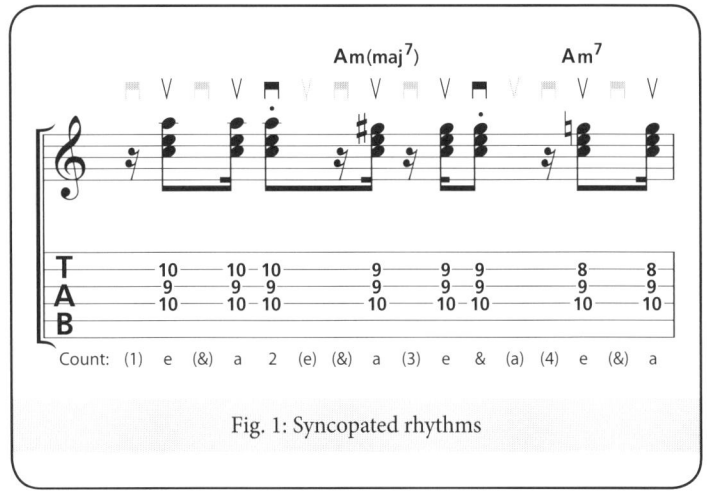

Fig. 1: Syncopated rhythms

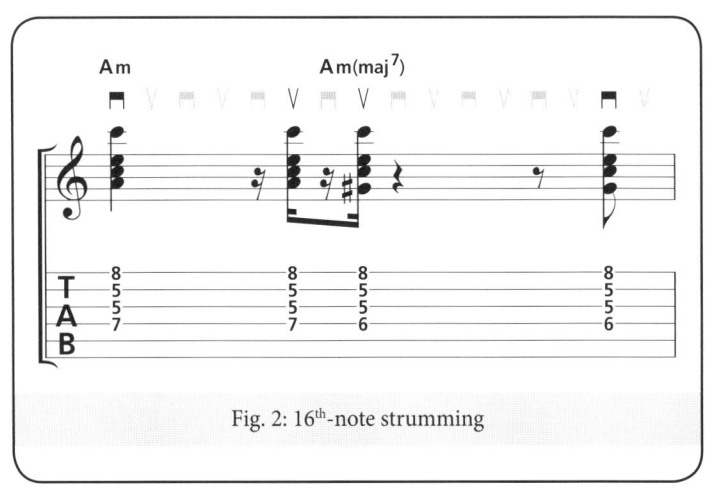

Fig. 2: 16th-note strumming

Technical Exercises

In this section the assessor will ask you to play a selection of exercises drawn from each of the five groups shown below. Groups A, B, C and D contain examples of the scales and modes, arpeggios and chords you can use when playing the pieces. In Group E you will be asked to prepare *one* stylistic study from the three printed. The choice of stylistic study will determine the style of the Quick Study Piece.

You do not need to memorise the exercises (and can use the book in the assessment) but the assessor will be looking for the speed of your response. The assessor will also give credit for the level of your musicality.

Before you start the section you will be asked whether you would like to play the exercises along with the click or hear a single measure of click before you commence the test. The tempo is ♩= 100.

Group A: Scales
The candidate must prepare all five shapes in the keys of G and B. The assessor will ask for all five shapes in either key.

1. Minor pentatonic scale (G minor pentatonic shown)

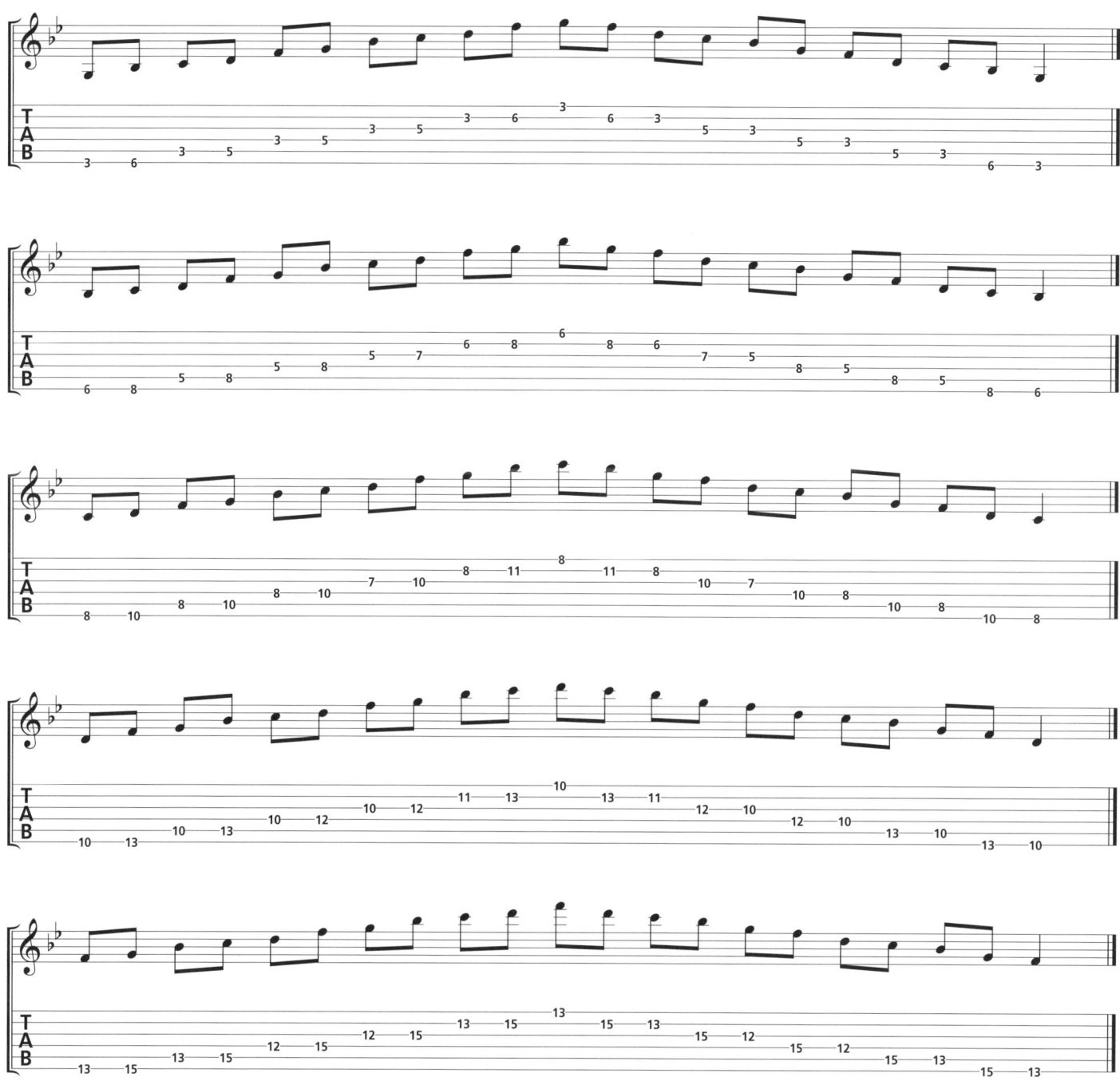

Technical Exercises

Group B: Modes
Two octaves, two positions. The first position is to be prepared on the E string from the starting notes of G–B chromatically. The second position is to be prepared on the A string from the starting notes of C–E chromatically.

1. Dorian (G dorian shown, root on E string)

2. Mixolydian (C mixolydian shown, root on A string)

Group C: Arpeggios
Two octaves, two positions. The first position is to be prepared on the E string from the starting notes of G–B chromatically. The second position is to be prepared on the A string from the starting notes of C–E chromatically.

1. Major7 arpeggios (A major7 shown, root on E string)

2. Minor7 arpeggios (C minor7 shown, root on A string)

3. Dominant7 arpeggios (D7 shown, root on A string)

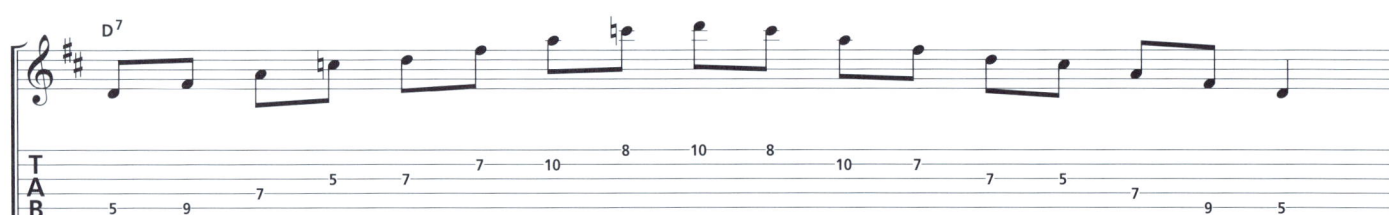

Technical Exercises

Group D: Chords

Two positions. The first position is to be prepared on the E string from the starting notes of G–B chromatically. The second position is to be prepared on the A string from the starting notes of C–E chromatically. Chords should be strummed and then picked (arpeggiated).

1. Minor $^{7\flat 5}$ (G minor $^{7\flat 5}$ shown, root on E string)

2. Diminished ^{7} (C diminished ^{7} shown, root on A string)

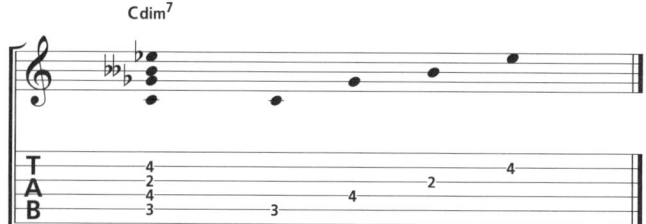

Group E: Stylistic Studies

You will prepare a technical study from one group of styles from the list below. Your choice of style will determine the style of the Quick Study Piece.

1. Rock/Metal: tapping and legato phrasing

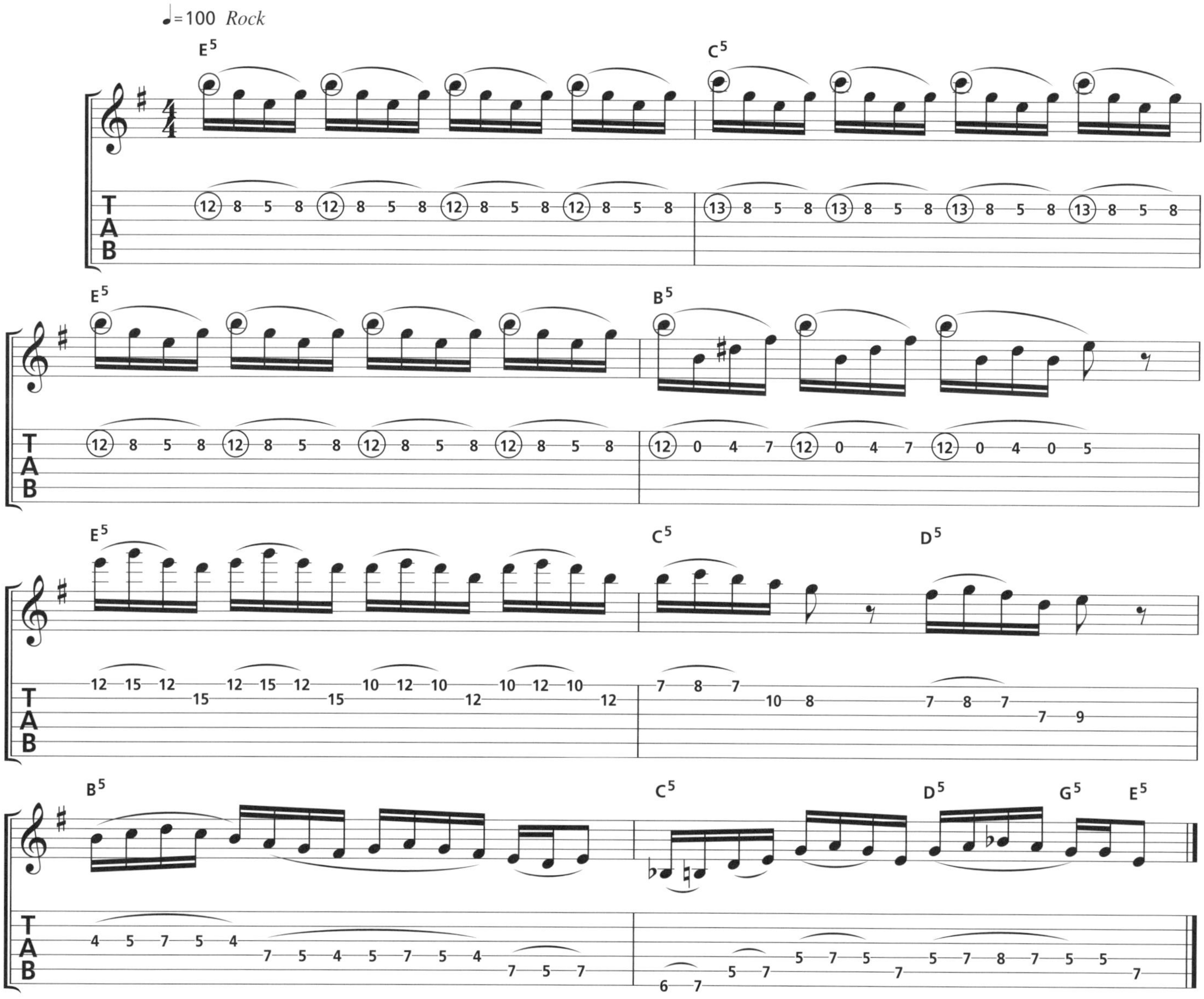

Technical Exercises

2. Funk: staccato phrasing and 16th-note strumming

3. Jazz/Latin/Blues: string bends and double-stops

Quick Study Piece

At this level/grade you will be asked to prepare and play a short Quick Study Piece (QSP). Printed below are three examples of the type of QSP you are likely to receive in the assessment. You will be shown the test and played the track with the *notated parts played*. Any measures that require improvisation will not be demonstrated. You will then have three minutes to study the test. The backing track will be played twice more. You will be allowed to practise during the first playing of the backing track, with the notated parts now absent, before playing it to the assessor on the second playing of the backing track.

The style of your QSP is determined by the stylistic study you selected in the technical exercise section. The QSP is in the form of a lead sheet and it is up to you to create your own interpretation of the music in the parts marked for improvisation.

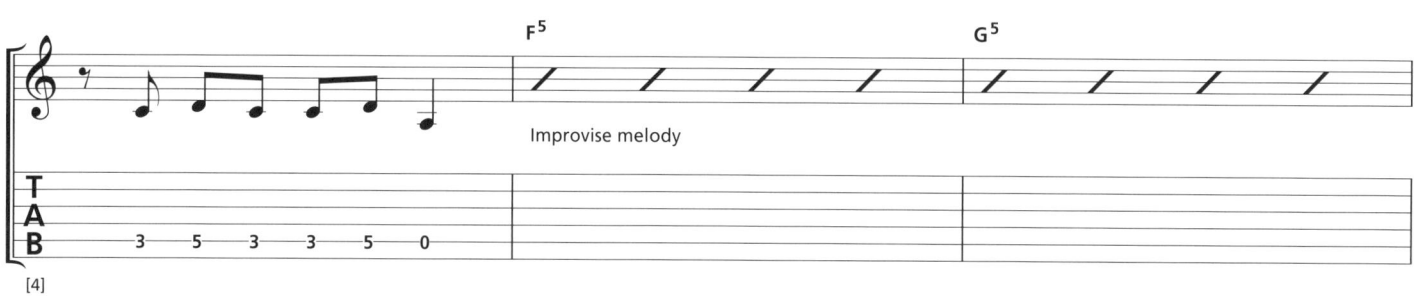

Quick Study Piece

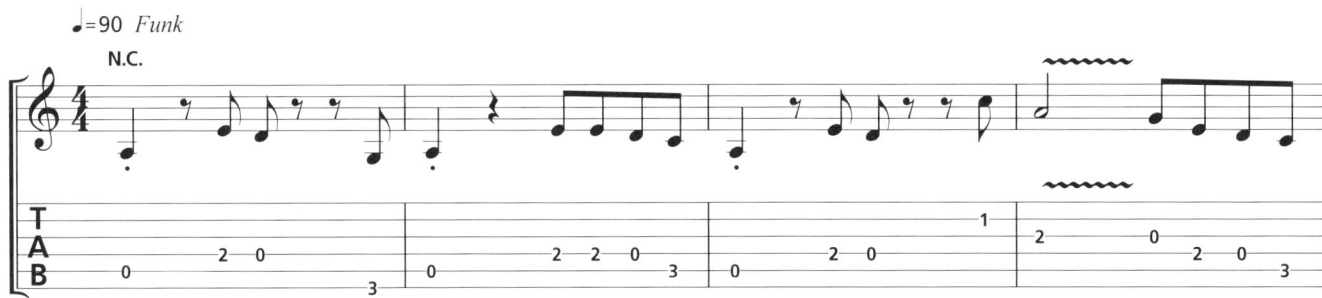

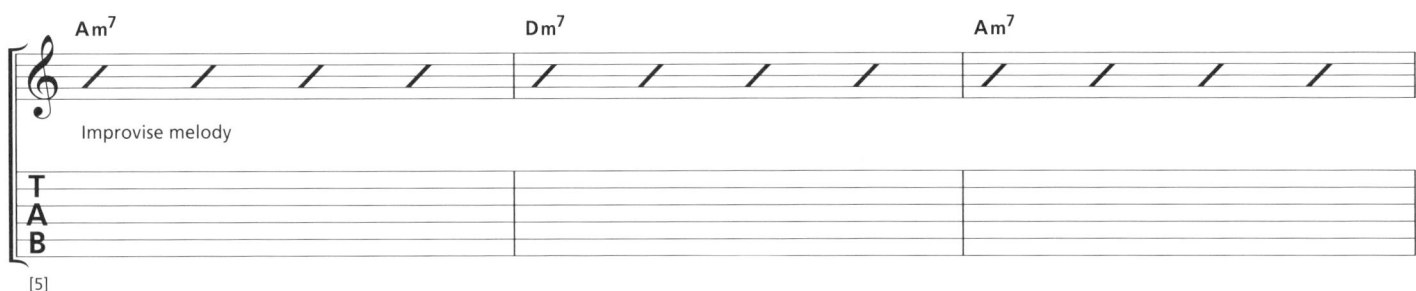

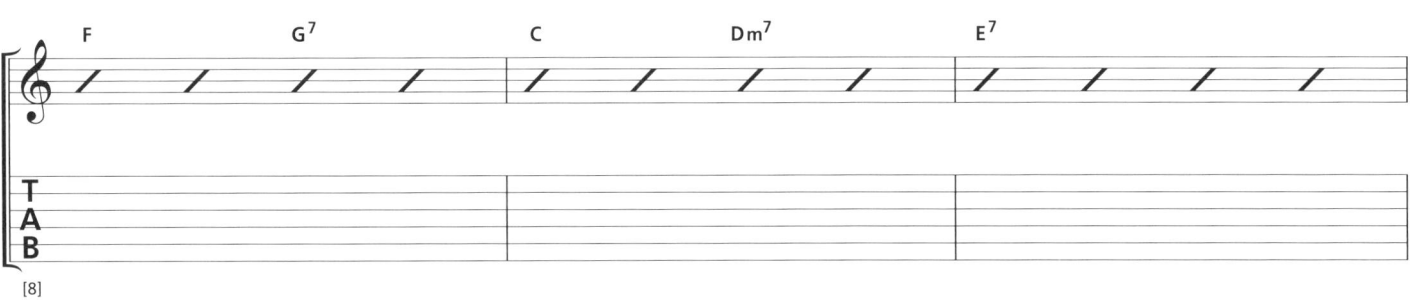

Quick Study Piece

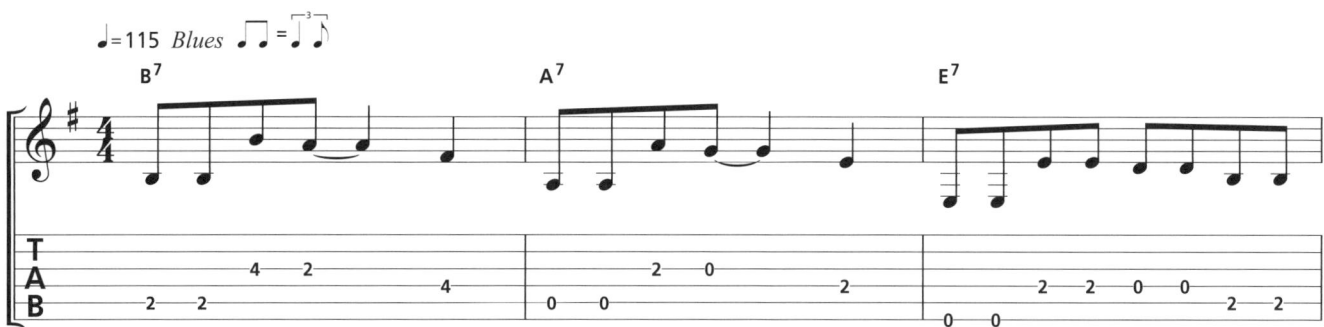
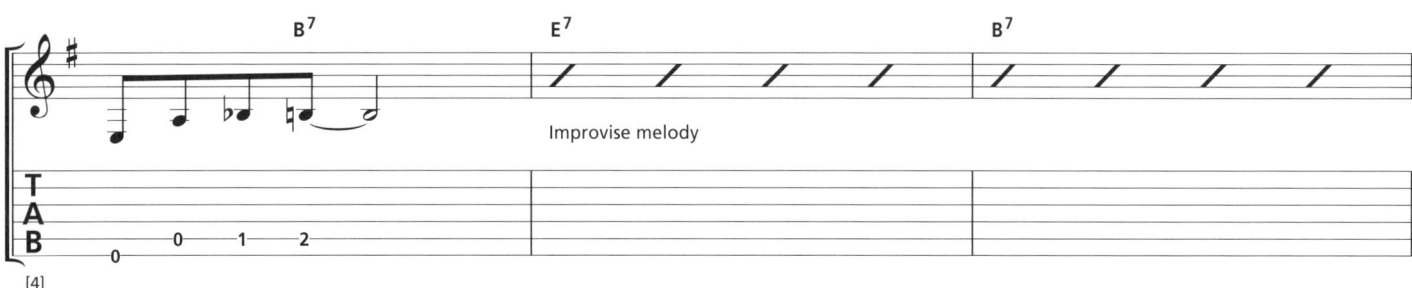
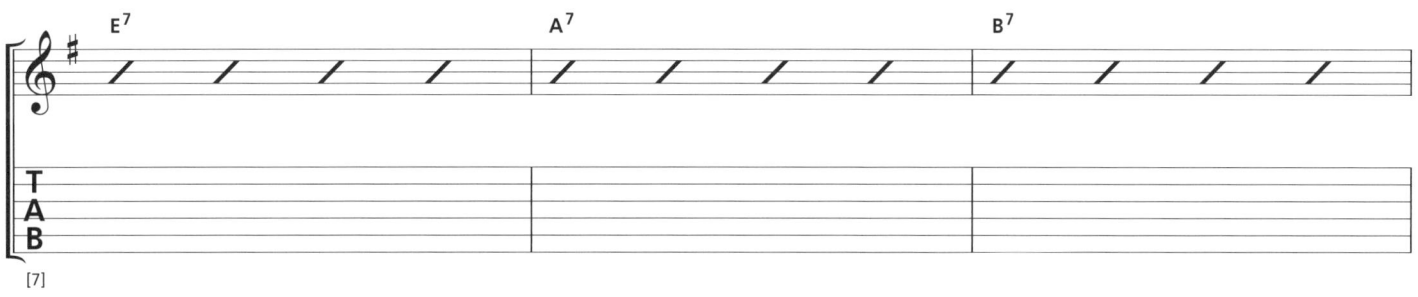
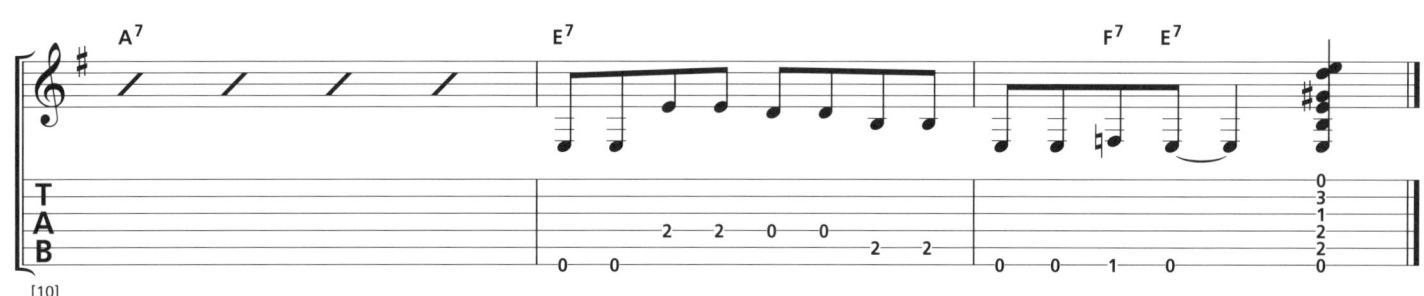

Ear Tests

There are two Ear Tests in this level/grade. The assessor will play each test to you twice. You will find one example of each type of test printed below.

Test 1: Melodic Recall
The assessor will play you a two measure melody with a bass and drum backing using either the D major pentatonic, D minor pentatonic or G natural minor scales. The first note of the melody will be *either* the root note *or* fifth and the first interval will be *either* ascending *or* descending. You will play the melody back on your instrument. You will hear the test twice.

Each time the test is played the sequence is: count-in, root note, count-in, melody. There will be a short gap for you to practise after you have heard the test for the second time. You will hear the count-in and root note for the third time followed by a *vocal* count-in and you will then play the melody to the bass and drum backing. The tempo is ♩= 90.

Test 2: Harmonic Recall
The assessor will play you a tonic chord followed by a four measure chord sequence in the key of D major played to a bass and drum backing. The sequence will use the I, ii, iii, IV, V and vi chords and will incorporate a dominant ^{7} (V^7) chord. You will be asked to play the chord sequence to the bass and drum backing in the rhythm shown in the example below. This rhythm will be used in all examples of this test given in the assessment. You will then be asked to identify the sequence you have played to the assessor, including any chord extensions. You will hear the test twice.

Each time the test is played the sequence is: count-in, tonic, count-in, chords. There will be a short gap for you to practise after you have heard the test for the second time. You will hear the count-in and tonic for the third time followed by a *vocal* count-in and you will then play the chords to the bass and drum backing. You should then name the chord sequence, including the chord type and any extensions. The tempo is ♩= 90.

General Musicianship Questions

In this part of the assessment you will be asked five questions. Four of these questions will be about general music knowledge and the fifth question asked will be about your instrument.

Music Knowledge

The assessor will ask you four music knowledge questions based on a piece of music that you have played in the assessment. You will nominate the piece of music about which the questions will be asked. In this level/grade you will be asked to demonstrate your answers on your instrument as directed by the assessor.

In Level/Grade 6 you will be asked:

- The names of pitches

- Any expressive musical marking found in the piece such as palm muting, accents, staccato, legato, vibrato

- Any dynamic marking found in the piece

- One type of scale that can be used appropriately in the solo section of the piece you have played and its relation to the underlying harmony of the piece

Instrument Knowledge

The assessor will also ask you one question regarding your instrument.

In Level/Grade 6 you will be asked to explain and demonstrate:

- Where to find the same pitch on two different strings

- The function of the volume and tone controls on your guitar

- The set up for the tone required for the piece you have played on the amp

- How to achieve changes in tone in a song

Further Information

Tips on how to approach this part of this assessment can be found in the *Syllabus Guide* for guitar, the Rockschool *Guitar Companion Guide* and on the Rockschool website: *www.rslawards.com*. The Introduction to Tone, a comprehensive explanation of guitar tones, can be found at the back of each level/grade book and the tone guide to each piece is in the appropriate Walkthrough.

Entering Rockschool Assessments

Entering a Rockschool assessment is easy, just go online and follow our simple six step process. All details for entering online, dates, fees, regulations and Free Choice pieces can be found at *www.rslawards.com*

- All candidates should ensure they bring their own Level/Grade syllabus book to the assessment or have proof of digital purchase ready to show the assessor.

- All Level/Grade 6–8 candidates must ensure that they bring valid photo ID to their assessment.

Marking Schemes

DEBUT TO LEVEL/GRADE 5 *

ELEMENT	PASS	MERIT	DISTINCTION
Performance Piece 1	12–14 out of 20	15–17 out of 20	18+ out of 20
Performance Piece 2	12–14 out of 20	15–17 out of 20	18+ out of 20
Performance Piece 3	12–14 out of 20	15–17 out of 20	18+ out of 20
Technical Exercises	9–10 out of 15	11–12 out of 15	13+ out of 15
Sight Reading *or* Improvisation & Interpretation	6 out of 10	7–8 out of 10	9+ out of 10
Ear Tests	6 out of 10	7–8 out of 10	9+ out of 10
General Musicianship Questions	3 out of 5	4 out of 5	5 out of 5
TOTAL MARKS	60%+	74%+	90%+

LEVELS/GRADES 6–8

ELEMENT	PASS	MERIT	DISTINCTION
Performance Piece 1	12–14 out of 20	15–17 out of 20	18+ out of 20
Performance Piece 2	12–14 out of 20	15–17 out of 20	18+ out of 20
Performance Piece 3	12–14 out of 20	15–17 out of 20	18+ out of 20
Technical Exercises	9–10 out of 15	11–12 out of 15	13+ out of 15
Quick Study Piece	6 out of 10	7–8 out of 10	9+ out of 10
Ear Tests	6 out of 10	7–8 out of 10	9+ out of 10
General Musicianship Questions	3 out of 5	4 out of 5	5 out of 5
TOTAL MARKS	60%+	74%+	90%+

PERFORMANCE CERTIFICATES | DEBUT TO LEVEL/GRADE 8 *

ELEMENT	PASS	MERIT	DISTINCTION
Performance Piece 1	12–14 out of 20	15–17 out of 20	18+ out of 20
Performance Piece 2	12–14 out of 20	15–17 out of 20	18+ out of 20
Performance Piece 3	12–14 out of 20	15–17 out of 20	18+ out of 20
Performance Piece 4	12–14 out of 20	15–17 out of 20	18+ out of 20
Performance Piece 5	12–14 out of 20	15–17 out of 20	18+ out of 20
TOTAL MARKS	60%+	75%+	90%+

* Note that there are no Debut Vocal assessments.

Introduction to Tone

A large part of an effective guitar performance is selecting the right tone. The electric guitar's sound is subject to a wide range of variables, and this guide outlines the basic controls present on most amplifiers as well as the common variations between models. There is also a basic overview of pickups and the effect their location on the guitar has on tone. Finally, it covers the differences between the types of distortion, which is crucial to getting your basic sound right.

At Level/Grade 6 the tone may change within the course of a piece. You should aim to use a tone that is stylistically appropriate and you may bring your own equipment to the assessment room for this purpose. There is a tone guide at the start of each Walkthrough to help you.

Basic amplifier controls

Most amplifiers come with a standard set of controls that are the same as, or very similar to, the diagram below. It's important to understand what each control is and the effect that it has on your guitar's tone.

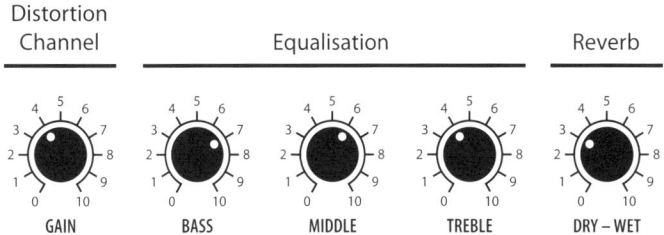

- **Channel (Clean/Distortion)**
  Most amplifiers have two channels that can be selected either by a switch on the amp or a footswitch. One channel is usually 'clean' while the other can be driven harder to create a distorted (or 'dirty') tone. If your amp doesn't have two channels, look at the 'variation of basic controls' below to see how to get clean and dirty tones from a one channel amp.

- **Gain**
  In simple terms, the gain determines how hard you drive the amp. This governs how distorted the dirty (also called 'drive', 'overdrive', or 'distortion') channel is and acts as a second volume control on the clean channel (though a high gain setting will distort even the clean channel).

- **Bass**
  This adjusts the lowest frequencies. Boost it to add warmth and reduce or 'cut' it if your sound is muddy or woolly.

- **Middle**
  This is the most important equalisation (often shortened to just 'EQ') control. Most of the guitar's tonal character is found in the mid-range so adjusting this control has a lot of impact upon your tone. Boosting it with a dirty sound will create a more classic rock tone while cutting it will produce a more metal one.

- **Treble**
  This adjusts the high frequencies. Boost it to add brightness and cut it if the sound is too harsh or brittle.

- **Reverb**
  Short for 'reverberation'. This artificially recreates the ambience of your guitar in a large room, usually a hall. This dial controls the balance between the 'dry' (the sound without the reverb) and 'wet' (the sound with the reverb) sounds.

Variations of basic controls

The diagram above shows the most common amp controls. There are many variations to this basic setup, which can often be confusing. The following section is a breakdown of some of the other amp controls you may encounter:

- **Presence control**
  Sometimes this dial replaces the 'middle' control and other times it appears in addition to it. It adjusts the higher mid-range frequencies (those found between the 'middle' and 'treble' dials).

- **No reverb control**
  Reverb can be a nice addition to your guitar tone but it's not essential. Don't be concerned if your amp doesn't have a reverb control.

- **Volume, gain, master setup**
  Single channel amplifiers often have an extra volume control (in addition to the master volume) located next to the gain control. For clean sounds, keep the gain set low and the volume similarly low and use the master control for overall volume. If the master control is on 10 and you require more level, turn the volume control up. However, you may find that this starts to distort as you reach the higher numbers.

  To get a distorted tone, turn the volume down low and the gain up until you get the amount of distortion you require. Regulate the overall level with master volume. If the master control is on 10 and you require more level simply turn the volume up. In this case, however, you may find you lose clarity before you reach maximum.

Pickups

Entire books have been devoted to the intricacies of pickups. However, three basic pieces of information will help you understand a lot about your guitar tone:

- **Singlecoils**
  These narrow pickups are fitted to many guitars. The Fender Stratocaster is the most famous guitar fitted with singlecoils. They produce a bright, cutting sound that can sound a little thin in some situations, especially heavier styles of rock music.

- **Humbuckers**
  This type of pickup was originally designed to remove or 'buck' the hum produced by singlecoil pickups, hence the name. They produce a warm, mellow sound compared to singlecoil pickups but have a tendency to sound a little muddy in some situations. They are usually identifiable because they are twice the width of a singlecoil pickup. The Gibson Les Paul is a well-known guitar fitted with humbucking pickups.

- **Pickup location**
  Basically, pickups located near the guitar's neck will have the warmest sound and those located near the bridge will have the brightest sound.

Different types of 'dirty' tones

There are lots of different words to describe the 'dirty' guitar sounds. In fact, all the sounds are 'distortions' of the clean tone, which can be confusing when you consider there's a 'type' of distortion called 'distortion'. Below is a simplified breakdown of the three main types of dirty sounds, plus some listening material to help you through this tonal minefield:

- **Overdrive**
  This is the 'mildest' form of distortion. It can be quite subtle and only evident when the guitar is played strongly. It can also be full-on and aggressive.
  Hear it on: Cream – 'Sunshine Of Your Love', AC/DC – 'Back In Black', Oasis – 'Cigarettes and Alcohol'.

- **Distortion**
  This is usually associated with heavier styles of music. It's dense and the most extreme of the dirty tones and is usually associated with heavy styles of music.
  Hear it on: Metallica – 'Enter Sandman', Avenged Sevenfold – 'Bat Country', Bon Jovi – 'You Give Love A Bad Name'.

- **Fuzz**
  As the name implies, fuzz is a broken, 'fuzzy' sound. It was popular in the 1960s but, while still evident in certain genres, it's less common now.
  Hear it on: Jimi Hendrix Experience – 'Purple Haze', The Kinks – 'You Really Got Me'.

Guitar Notation Explained

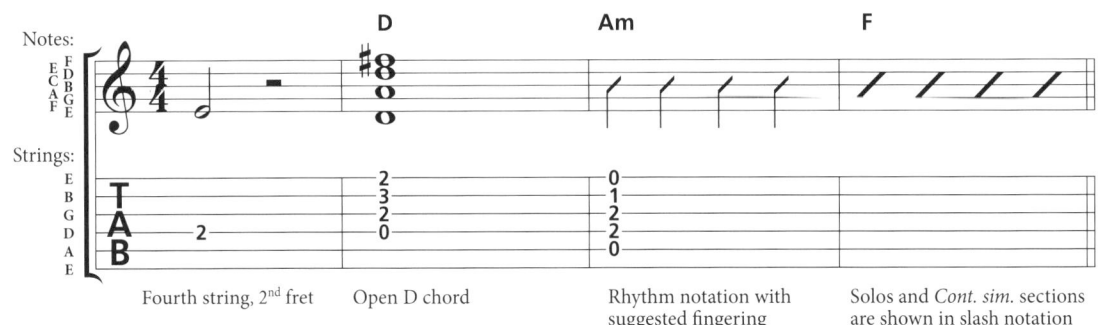

THE MUSICAL STAVE shows pitches and rhythms and is divided by lines into measures. Pitches are named after the first seven letters of the alphabet.

TABLATURE graphically represents the guitar fingerboard. Each horizontal line represents a string and each number represents a fret.

Fourth string, 2nd fret | Open D chord | Rhythm notation with suggested fingering | Solos and *Cont. sim.* sections are shown in slash notation

Definitions For Special Guitar Notation

HAMMER-ON: Pick the lower note, then sound the higher note by fretting it without picking.

PULL-OFF: Pick the higher note then sound the lower note by lifting the finger without picking.

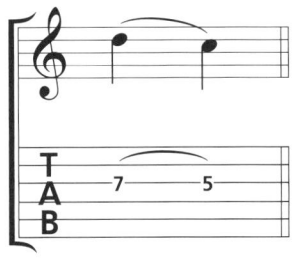

SLIDE: Pick the first note and slide to the next. If the line connects (as below) the second note is *not* repicked.

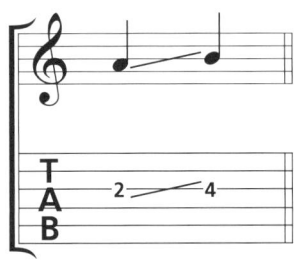

GLISSANDO: Slide off of a note at the end of its rhythmic value. The note that follows *is* repicked.

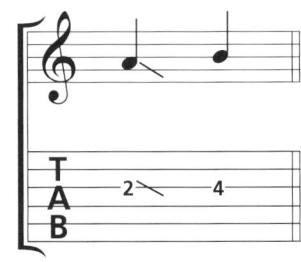

STRING BENDS: Pick the first note then bend (or release the bend) to the pitch indicated in brackets.

VIBRATO: Vibrate the note by bending and releasing the string smoothly and continuously.

TRILL: Rapidly alternate between the two bracketed notes by hammering on and pulling off.

NATURAL HARMONICS: Lightly touch the string above the indicated fret then pick to sound a harmonic.

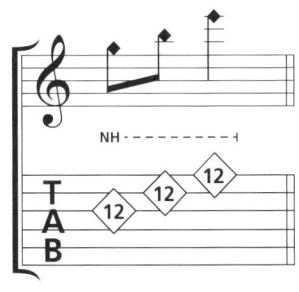

PINCHED HARMONICS: Bring the thumb of the picking hand into contact with the string immediately after the pick.

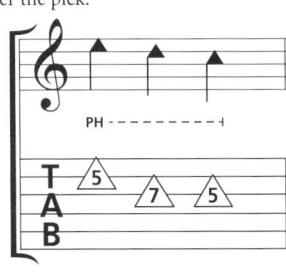

PICK-HAND TAP: Strike the indicated note with a finger from the picking hand. Usually followed by a pull-off.

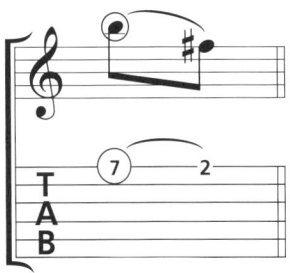

FRET-HAND TAP: As pick-hand tap, but use fretting hand. Usually followed by a pull-off or hammer-on.

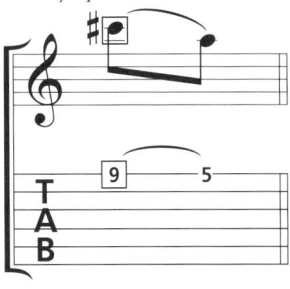

QUARTER-TONE BEND: Pick the note indicated and bend the string up by a quarter tone.

PRE-BENDS: Before picking the note, bend the string from the fret indicated between the staves, to the equivalent pitch indicated in brackets in the TAB.

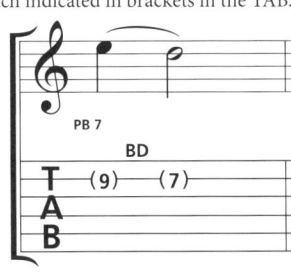

WHAMMY BAR BEND: Use the whammy bar to bend notes to the pitches indicated in brackets in the TAB.

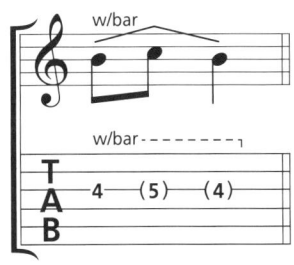

D.%. al Coda

D.C. al Fine

- Go back to the sign (%), then play until the measure marked **To Coda** ⊕ then skip to the section marked ⊕ **Coda**.

- Go back to the beginning of the song and play until the measure marked **Fine** (end).

- Repeat the measures between the repeat signs.

- When a repeated section has different endings, play the first ending only the first time and the second ending only the second time.

Mechanical Copyright Information

Cramp Your Style
(Hale)
EMI Music Publishing Limited

If I Ain't Got U
(Cook)
EMI Music Publishing Limited

The Real Thing
(Scott/Davis/Toby/Boyd/Harris)
Universal/MCA Music Limited/EMI Music Publishing Limited/BMG Rights Management (UK) Limited

I Wanna Be Your Lover
(Nelson)
Universal/MCA Music Limited

Crossroads
(Johnson/Clapton)
Eric Clapton

Fell On Black Days
(Cornell)
BMG Rights Management (UK) Limited

mcps

INTRODUCING...
rockschool®

POPULAR MUSIC THEORY

The *essential* guide for rock & pop musicians

GRADES DEBUT–8

OUT NOW!

Discover more at
www.rslawards.com/theory

Enter online at
www.rslawards.com/enter-online